About the co-author
Tony Jimenez

My golfing 'wow' moment arrived as a young child. Sitting in my grandparents' living room, watching on a grainy old black-and-white TV set, I was entranced by this shadowy figure reacting with stunned surprise after delivering a hole-in-one. It was, I discovered, the first time that particular feat had been televised live in Britain. That magical stroke by Tony Jacklin sparked my interest in the game. I eventually went on to fulfil my dream of becoming a sports journalist and ended up making a special friend of that shadowy figure who popped up on our screen in September 1967. To you 'Sir Tony', thanks a million for affording me the honour and privilege of helping to compile this account of a remarkable Ryder Cup career.

Tony Jacklin:
My Ryder Cup Journey

Tony Jacklin and Tony Jimenez

Tony Jacklin:
My Ryder Cup Journey

Pegasus

A CIP catalogue record for this title is
available from the British Library

ISBN-978 1 91090 363 9

Pegasus is an imprint of
Pegasus Elliot MacKenzie Publishers Ltd.
www.pegasuspublishers.com

First Published in 2021

Pegasus
Sheraton House Castle Park
Cambridge CB3 0AX England

Printed & Bound in Great Britain

Dedication

To ensure this great game of ours survives and thrives in perpetuity, I would like to urge all you golfers out there—professionals, amateurs and weekend hackers alike—to protect and respect the core elements that make it such a fantastic sport.

The new, first-of-its-kind Nicklaus-Jacklin Award presented by Aon, which commemorates the famous last-hole concession from my halved Ryder Cup match with Jack in 1969, is an example of the virtues that he and I hold dear.

At every Ryder Cup, the honour will go to one player from each team who best embodies the competition, who sees the bigger picture and makes the better decisions critical to sportsmanship, teamwork and performance.

The award is inspired by the decisions of yesterday and defines the decisions of today.

Contents

Foreword

Tony Jacklin changed the Ryder Cup forever.

When he began captaining the European team in the 1980s, he forced the Americans to take a step back and realise: "These guys across the pond can really play."

The Europeans' narrow loss at Palm Beach Gardens in 1983 started their positive momentum. Most of the European players were dejected after the loss – with the exception of Seve Ballesteros as well as Jacklin himself. Their response was: "No, no, this is good because we know we can beat the Americans now. We are as good as they are or maybe even better."

Tony paved the way for European team golf and the Ryder Cup being the enormous global spectacle it is today. The history of Jacklin's four matches as captain in 1983, 1985, 1987 and 1989 was the prelude to what has been over thirty years of European dominance in the Ryder Cup.

When I was appointed American captain for the 2008 matches at Valhalla, I was determined to shake things up, and I used some of Tony's tactics and strategies to give our team any edge possible. We had been beaten three successive times in 2002, 2004 and 2006, and I didn't want a fourth on my watch.

Tony's a wise man who knows a lot about the history of golf and the Ryder Cup. For Americans, it's in our heads, but to him, it's different; it's part of his DNA.

When I made my debut as a player at The Belfry in 1989, he was an intimidating presence for me. His self-belief stood out, he trusted his players, and he made sure they were fully motivated. He was the first captain to have a major say in how the host course was set up, which was a big influence on me in 2008.

The Europeans always had a really cohesive bunch of players under his leadership. They tended to have small groups who stayed in tight units, and I went for a similar approach when I brought in my pod system in 2008. For the Europeans, that was a natural thing — the English would play together, the Swedes, the Spaniards, the Irish.

Tony's teams were a very united bunch and a hard outfit to beat. Most of his side are now in the Hall of Fame, legendary figures in the history of our sport. They were totally single-minded when it came to the Ryder Cup, just loaded with self-belief, and I guarantee that spirit was forged by Tony.

We adopted many different systems to pick our teams, which was one of the first things I questioned when I became captain. Much like Tony before me, I was desperate to have the best players on my side.

It really struck a nerve when Tony led Europe to their first-ever win on US soil at Muirfield Village in 1987. It's true to say that the Ryder Cup has grown out of proportion since, but to me, it was massive even back then. When we were greeted at the airport by hundreds of European fans in 1989, we felt like rock stars. They were cheering and welcoming us; it was incredible. When the time came to do battle out on the course, I felt the most pressure I'd ever felt in my life.

It got your nerves to the point where you were shaking in desperation to succeed. The emotions were ramped up, and I promise you that Tony Jacklin started much of that with his influence, his leadership and his passion.

Paul Azinger, 2021

Chapter 1
Cancer

I used to think I was immortal when I was trotting around the globe in my golfing pomp, flying here, there and everywhere chasing my dream of becoming the best player on the planet.

If world rankings had existed in that era, I would almost certainly have occupied the number-one slot after I had followed up my victory in the 1969 Open at Royal Lytham by winning the 1970 US Open at Hazeltine National.

Now, sitting here in my Florida home in my mid-seventies, I can smile wistfully at the mirror, knowing that I've had to dodge a few curveballs in my time as far as health issues are concerned.

I need to wear two hi-tech hearing aids every day due to being profoundly deaf; I suffer from dangerous sleep apnoea — which means my breathing stops and starts at night — and I've been undergoing treatment for cancer on and off for the past five years.

My wife Astrid sprang a surprise by organising a seventieth birthday party for me at The Belfry — the iconic Ryder Cup venue — in Sutton Coldfield in July 2014. More than ninety guests were there, family and a few friends, including Jack Nicklaus, who was in town for the Wimbledon tennis and The Open, and it was around that time that I felt a lump in my groin region.

I thought it might be a hernia at first. I'd had a double hernia when I was a baby, and that was the first thing that went through my mind. I booked in for a hospital scan, but it took quite a while to get a diagnosis.

Eventually, I had a biopsy and, when the results came back around Christmas that year, I was told I had follicular lymphoma.

The doctors said it was incurable but manageable with the correct treatment, adding the proviso that it can also turn into something more serious in ten per cent of cases.

The first thing I did was call a golf-mad Scottish friend of mine, Dr Ian Hay, for advice. Straight away, he said I should book myself an appointment at the Mayo Clinic in Minnesota with Tom Habermann, who apparently was the number-one oncologist expert on lymphoma.

Astrid and I jumped on a plane the next day, flew up there for a second opinion, and he confirmed the original findings. Although it was all deadly serious and obviously extremely worrying, looking back, it's funny to recall what happened while I was waiting for his diagnosis.

Dr Habermann, I was quickly finding out, was also a big golf fan. While I'm anxiously fretting as I wait to discover if I'm going to live or die, I have to listen to three long-winded stories about the great Ben Hogan before he gets to the bottom line.

Finally, he said, "If you've got to have lymphoma, you've got the best version of it. You won't die OF it; you'll die WITH it." Phew, what a relief!

After getting home to Florida, I received four one-litre infusions of Rituximab over one month. This is a medication given for several hours via a slow injection into the veins.

Clearly, Minnesota is a fair old way from Florida, so I needed to enlist the services of a local oncologist, and I found an Indian guy by the name of Dr Manjesh Lingamurthy.

I continued having CAT scans and PET scans so that the specialists could determine the severity of the lymphoma. The Rituximab was doing its job, but a bit of a conflict arose between my two oncologists.

Dr Lingamurthy wanted to include an element of chemotherapy in the injections, but Dr Habermann was against the idea, saying the Rituximab was working fine on its own. He was proved right; I started to feel better, and all I needed to do was get checked out every six months.

Then, suddenly, at Christmas 2019, my left ankle started to swell up — the cancer had returned. This time I did need chemo with the

Rituximab, six sessions over six months. *"Shit"*, I thought, *"that's not what I want to hear."*

Even though everything was going through Dr Habermann, I again decided to avoid travelling all the way to Minnesota and chose to have the treatment in Florida.

On day one, I had six hours of Rituximab and chemo before going back on day two for only chemo. After a couple of weeks, my ankle started to get back to its normal size, so I could tell it was working.

I repeated the treatment a month after the first infusions, and the specialists sent me in for more scans and a biopsy to make sure the lymphoma hadn't mutated into a different cancer.

It transpired that the combination of Rituximab and chemo was working as it should. I went on to have the third and fourth bouts of treatment, after which the oncologists said it had all gone so well, I wouldn't need the fifth and sixth sessions.

Although both doctors were fully involved in the process, I always put Dr Habermann first in terms of advice. To try and make sure I kept Dr Lingamurthy onside, I took a signed copy of my fictional book *Bad Lies* to his clinic, dedicated it to him in a short note along with the words, "Thanks for everything you do".

An hour later he called me to say thanks. But he kept asking, "Are you Tony, Tony the golfer?"

You see, every time I had visited him, he called me Anthony and this time the penny finally dropped.

Previously, he had no idea I was the man who'd won two Majors and led Europe to Ryder Cup glory. It was another amusing moment because suddenly he was all over me like a rash, wanting to talk about golf, and I couldn't get off the phone.

The most important thing, though, was the cancer was now in remission. The doctors explained that I would continue to need regular check-ups and regularly monitor myself, but it could be that I wouldn't need treatment again for another five or ten years.

I feel blessed in many ways. Some people much less fortunate than me are given the horrible news they only have three months or six months to live and that's a thought that often runs through my mind.

I feel lucky that my disorder is not life-threatening although it could have been if I hadn't taken care of it. We all need to be vigilant when it comes to health and get ourselves checked if something is concerning us.

My mother should have lived a lot longer. She died at the age of seventy with stomach cancer because she refused to see anyone about it. By the time doctors operated on her, it was too late.

My father also had colon cancer and I need checks for that too every seven years or so. I don't smoke but I do drink and I don't know how I would cope without my regular glass of Glenmorangie or a gin and tonic or two.

Dad did have treatment and he lived to the age of seventy-nine. He came to live with us in Florida for a while, after my mum had died, before deciding he wanted to go home to Scunthorpe and that was where he eventually passed away.

If I had a wish now it would be that I was more supple than I am. I don't enjoy golf as I should because I'm so stiff all the time and I can't get my club back far enough in the swing. I struggle with my flexibility, but I guess that's what comes with old age.

Just before I was first diagnosed with cancer, Astrid noticed that something was amiss with my breathing at night, so I booked myself in for a full three-day medical at the Mayo Clinic.

They hooked me up to a load of machines, monitored my sleep for six hours and found out that I stopped breathing forty times in one hour for thirty seconds at a time — and that's bloody dangerous.

I was diagnosed with sleep apnoea and told that I would need to wear a special contraption whenever I sleep in order to deal with it. The machine allows a constant stream of air through small caps I put in my nose.

Again, I was lucky that Astrid noticed I had an issue because I was asleep and didn't have a clue. It's a pain in the backside taking this contraption everywhere I go. It comes in a holdall and the aviation authorities don't include it as hand luggage on a plane because it's deemed a medical necessity.

Sometimes when I go back to England, I need an adaptor and an extension lead in case the power supply is a long way from the bed.

There's a tub in the machine that needs to be filled with distilled water. Keeping the whole unit germ-free is a bit of a palaver because all the tubes are in constant use and need regular cleaning. But without the diagnosis I received, who knows what could have happened?

All that gasping for air at night can cause death. It's an age-related condition for most but if any of you out there have a tendency to snore loudly, get yourself checked because that's often a sign of sleep apnoea.

When it comes to describing my deafness, I always feel indebted to the legendary Arnold Palmer. Twenty or so years ago he introduced me to Bill Austin, who comes from Minnesota and owns Starkey Hearing Technologies.

It's one of the biggest privately-owned hearing aid companies in the world and they do a wonderful job, visiting poor countries to help out kids.

I've had so many hearing aids over the years that weren't ideal, especially those that have to be worn outside the ear because here in Florida, when you play golf in the summer, the perspiration gets in.

The ones I wear now are very small but extremely powerful. They go inside the ear beyond the wax and as close to the eardrum as anything I've ever worn. The hearing aids have Bluetooth and when I watch TV, there's a special box under the screen that can put the sound on mute for everyone else while I can still hear.

I've had severe hearing problems for thirty-odd years. It puts the kybosh on restaurants and other noisy places. If there's background noise, I can't join in a conversation, and it's a real pain not being able to hear like everyone else.

I take my hearing aids out at night — a bomb could go off and it wouldn't faze me — but even with them in, my hearing is probably fifty per cent of normal. If people are talking to me from behind, I can't hear them. They often think I'm being rude, and Astrid has to explain things to them.

I go to Jack Nicklaus's Memorial Tournament in Dublin, Ohio every year for a round-table discussion with a lot of the old golfers — guys like Lee Trevino, Hale Irwin, Paul Azinger — but some of the time, I'm clueless over what is being said.

I apologise when I play golf with someone I don't know. I explain that I can't always hear and if I don't react to something they say, at least they'll know why.

The condition stems from an incident that occurred when I was about forty. I was back home in Lincolnshire with my cousin's husband, who was a farmer and a clay pigeon shot. I used to shoot pheasants in the 1960s and 1970s, but I never did clays.

One day he took me to shoot clays. I protested that I didn't have anything to cover my ears, but he said not to worry, I'd be all right. We went into this quarry and after we came out, I could hear what sounded like a million cats meowing in my ears.

The incessant noise gradually subsided after a few days, but the damage was done. I used to get in London taxis and cabbies would often start golf conversations, but I was good for nothing because I was staring at the back of their heads and couldn't hear a word.

I used to do a lot of flying but I've not had a proper conversation on a plane for thirty years because all the background noise makes it impossible.

The black hearing aids I wear are worth $5,000 a pair and they're invaluable. My hearing was a handicap when I had a stint on the US Seniors Tour but at least all the other players knew about it.

At night I always take them out before I brush my teeth and place them by the sink. There was a funny, if costly, moment a while back when I woke up in the morning and only one hearing aid was there.

Astrid always gets up much earlier than me. I asked her if she'd seen the missing one and she said "no". Then, she suddenly remembered she had risen early that morning when it was semi-dark. Thinking the cat had missed the litter tray that sits in the bathroom, she'd picked up this black thing she thought was something else (!) and flushed it down the toilet.

Of course, it was the missing hearing aid, and I was $2,500 worse off.

The health issues I've experienced in recent times have made me take stock of my life and golf career, especially the love affair I've always had with the Ryder Cup — hence this book.

I wanted to put on record the thoughts, feelings and emotions I went through in seven memorable matches as a player and four unforgettable matches as captain. Hopefully, the next few chapters will prove as enjoyable for you to read as they were for me to recall.

Testimonial from Sir Nick Faldo

Open wins: 1987, 1990, 1992
US Masters wins: 1989, 1990, 1996
Ryder Cup playing appearances: 1977, 1979, 1981, 1983, 1985, 1987,
1989, 1991, 1993, 1995, 1997
Ryder Cup captain: 2008

Tony was the working man's hero of British golf back in the 1960s and then became a trailblazer competing in America, which culminated in him winning The Open in 1969 and the US Open in 1970.

With the creation of the European Tour in the 1970s, Tony recognised the opportunity that if we did things right, or "first class" as he put it, that we could take on and beat America in the Ryder Cup.

I can't think of anyone who has given more heart, passion and soul to British and European golf on and off the fairways. And that's before we get to his contribution to the European team.

I'm pretty sure our run under Tony's captaincy and leadership in the 1980s is still fresh in many golf fans' minds. It quite simply was the spearhead to where we are today in the Ryder Cup.

Tony's Ryder Cup captaincy should be more than enough for him to be awarded a knighthood.

Chapter 2
1967 Matches

Foursomes: Morning

B Huggett & G Will halved with B Casper & J Boros

P Alliss & C O'Connor lost by 2 holes to A Palmer & G Dickinson

T Jacklin & D Thomas beat D Sanders & G Brewer 4 & 3

B Hunt & N Coles lost to R Nichols & J Pott 6 & 5

Foursomes: Afternoon:

B Huggett & G Will lost to B Casper & J Boros by 1 hole

M Gregson & H Boyle lost to G Dickinson & A Palmer 5 & 4

T Jacklin & D Thomas beat G Littler & A Geiberger 3 & 2

P Alliss & C O'Connor lost to R Nichols & J Pott 2 & 1

Fourballs: Morning

P Alliss & C O'Connor lost to B Casper & G Brewer 3 & 2

B Hunt & N Coles lost to R Nichols & J Pott by 1 hole

T Jacklin & D Thomas lost to G Littler & A Geiberger by 1 hole

B Huggett & G Will lost to G Dickinson & D Sanders 3 & 2

Fourballs: Afternoon:

B Hunt & N Coles lost to B Casper & G Brewer 5 & 3

P Alliss & M Gregson lost to G Dickinson & D Sanders 3 & 2

G Will & H Boyle lost to A Palmer & J Boros by 1 hole

T Jacklin & D Thomas halved with G Littler & A Geiberger

Singles: Morning

H Boyle lost to G Brewer 4 & 3

P Alliss lost to B Casper 2 & 1

T Jacklin lost to A Palmer 3 & 2

B Huggett beat J Boros by 1 hole

N Coles beat D Sanders 2 & 1

M Gregson lost to A Geiberger 4 & 2

D Thomas halved with G Littler

B Hunt halved with R Nichols

Singles: Afternoon:

B Huggett lost to A Palmer 5 & 3

P Alliss beat G Brewer 2 & 1

T Jacklin lost to G Dickinson 3 & 2

C O'Connor lost to R Nichols 3 & 2

G Will lost to J Pott 3 & 1

M Gregson lost to A Geiberger 2 & 1

B Hunt halved with J Boros

N Coles beat D Sanders 2 & 1

The friendships you create in the Ryder Cup can last a lifetime. I don't like comparing it to war, but you sometimes hear the old veterans saying that the sort of relationships built in times of real strife, the love you develop for your comrade is often stronger than the love between a man and a woman.

Going out to battle for each other, albeit on a golf course rather than a war field, you develop a deep mutual respect and there's a strong element of that in the Ryder Cup.

The camaraderie between the players, the tough matches, the hard times, the trials and tribulations all contribute to this feeling. You see guys in tears like you did with Seve Ballesteros and Nick Faldo at Oak Hill in 1995, both of them crying their eyes out.

I went through this seven times as a player and four times as the captain. When you're in charge, you try to be everyone's best friend. You can't tell them how to play because they wouldn't be there if they weren't the best players, but you try to protect them the best way you can. You feel for them when they get beaten and you are elated for them when they emerge triumphant.

In terms of team events, the Ryder Cup is the pinnacle. The World Cup of Golf has been around since 1953 but it pales in comparison.

The BBC's Peter Alliss — a fine player in his day — and I paired up in the two-man World Cup event a few times. I did my duty, but the teams involved were invariably weaker than they should have been. The Americans, for example, would often be represented by their fourth- and fifth-choice players.

It was run on the cheap and a bit of a farce to call it the World Cup. They would organise hotel accommodation and, if you preferred to stay in your own room rather than share with a teammate, you would have to pay for the privilege.

Back in Houston in 1967, for my very first Ryder Cup as a player, we were all given 10-gallon Texas Stetsons.

The Champions Golf Club, founded by Jimmy Demaret - the first three-time winner of the US Masters – and Jack Burke Junior ten years earlier, was a great venue. But the Great Britain players didn't have a team room in those days, so we were left to our own devices quite a bit. I was 23 years young and making my debut that week, as was the Leicester-born Malcolm Gregson, and we hung out together for those matches.

The linchpin of the American team was the inimitable Arnold Palmer, and he decided to play silly buggers and take some of us up in an aeroplane on the last practice day: me, Jimmy Demaret, my teammate George Will and Royal Birkdale professional Bobby Halsall.

He didn't mess around, we dipped, dived and criss-crossed in the sky - it was a real daredevil trip.

We flew over the golf course at 1,000-feet, flat out, twisting one way and then the other. George peed his pants and I still don't know to this day why I didn't, too. It was terrible and, when it was over, Palmer's full-time pilot Darryl Walsh was summoned to the phone to speak to the local air traffic controller.

Darryl was making all sorts of excuses before Palmer, to his eternal credit, grabbed the phone to make clear that it was he himself who had been at the wheel and that Darryl was not at fault.

Palmer was grovelling, saying, "Yes sir, no sir, three bags full, sir," and it was quite something in those days to see the man known as the 'King' acting like that.

But had it not been for Demaret, who also had his own plane and liked flying, Palmer may have lost his licence. Demaret wrote a letter to the authorities and nothing serious ever came of the incident.

Dai Rees was our captain that week and nine-times Major winner Ben Hogan was the American skipper. There was no love lost between Hogan and Palmer.

Hogan, famously, never took any prisoners and I remember hearing a locker-room story involving Palmer and a teammate in which the pair of them were discussing whether to play with the larger American-style ball or the smaller one that was more familiar to us Britons.

Apparently, Hogan turned around at one point and snapped at Palmer: "Who said you were playing anyway?"

It was the sort of put-down that he loved to deliver. It tended to be a battle of egos between the two of them.

Hogan was revered by the players on that 1967 US team. Guys like Gay Brewer and Johnny Pott were fearful of him. There was a kind of feeling of, 'for Christ's sake Ben, don't come and watch me playing'.

At that stage of my career, I was playing a lot in the States. These guys were pals of mine, and I knew them well. If Hogan decided to pause in a speech, you would have heard a pin drop. He was 'The Man' and had everyone spellbound.

I paired up with Dave Thomas that week. We won 2½ points out of four in the foursomes and fourballs and did well.

Dave, though, had a bit of mental baggage because he had the yips big time with the chipper. Australian Peter Thomson, a five-time winner of The Open, played with him once and said there was an occasion when Dave's club stuck in the ground, his divot flew over the ball, and the ball went nowhere.

Dave, who twice finished second in The Open, really was atrocious with the chipper and did everything in his power not to have to chip the ball. He was all right out of bunkers. If he had to chip over sand, he would simply knock his ball into the trap and play from there. When it came to chipping, he would just freeze over the ball.

There were four par-5s and four par-3s at the Champions Golf Club, and Dave and I figured out a way to play in the foursomes — I would tee off at the par-5s and the par-3s, and if he missed the green, it would be up to me to do the chipping.

We 'ham and egged it' pretty well between the two of us but I recall one time when Dave was faced with a chip. He was over a bunker, and I was watching him because I knew how petrified he would be.

He took this huge backswing, twice as long as it needed to be, opened the face of his wedge to counteract the excess swing and hit this bloody thing that went way up into the air and, remarkably, the ball finished stone dead close to the cup.

We looked at each other and burst out laughing because we both knew it had been a complete fluke. Our record that week as a pair was brilliant, but I didn't exactly sparkle in the singles — losing both of them 3 & 2 to Palmer, and to that so-and-so Gardner Dickinson.

We had a young team that week and were hammered by a record margin: 23½ points to 8½. I often talk about the difference between confidence and bravado; that was definitely a bravado era for our players.

Dai was a good captain, a great guy and full of enthusiasm. He cared about making everyone feel as comfortable as possible. We all wanted to do as well as we could, but it really was quite impossible to talk about winning the overall contest.

We were soundly beaten, but it was a great experience for a 23-year-old. The camaraderie wasn't the same as it was in later years and you never say it of course, but it was a lost cause from the outset.

Our side were all pals, and we wanted the best for each other but there wasn't the same passion that I experienced when I was the captain in the 1980s. Belief is central to everything in any sport and that week, it was more about bravado than it was about proper, deep-set confidence.

Going back to my partnership with Dave. It was perfect for the two of us in the fourballs and foursomes because I was a good chipper and putter back then and Dave was a great driver.

Some people say you should put two players like that together in foursomes, though not in fourballs, but I've never believed that. Some people also say a long hitter should be paired with a short hitter. All that is a load of bull as far as I'm concerned. It's about spirit, togetherness and getting on well. Dave and I were confident in each other, and we came out on top more often than not that week.

We never discussed team strategies back then. We, as players, just did as we were told in terms of where we were put in the order of play. There was no team room like there is now so three or four of us would just wander into Houston and find a restaurant in the evening.

We played for a total of 32 points back then, but it's been 28 since 1979 and I can't stress enough how important the current format is.

I told the bigwigs when I stepped down as captain after the 1989 matches that there's one thing they should never change and that's the format of the competition.

It's so important for a captain to be able to leave four players out on the opening two days. You can hide players in the foursomes and fourballs who may not be firing on all cylinders and then tuck them into the middle order at four or five for the twelve last-day singles.

If you've got a weakness or two in your line-up, you can hide them and the Americans know the more matches they have, the better their chances of winning are. Once we hit on the current format, it was a tremendous thing for the competition because it produced so many nail-biting finishes.

Europe have dominated for the last thirty-or-so years, and you could be forgiven for thinking that the Ryder Cup has become a bit lopsided in our favour - it was anything but that in my time as captain. There were so many close matches that went down to the wire and the results could easily have been very different.

Palmer was in his pomp for those matches in Houston. It was like performing alongside Jesus Christ if you were playing with him. 'Arnie's Army' was a huge advantage for him, especially in America. His fans didn't give a stuff what you were doing, and you knew that all the way around.

He was a tough nut to crack back then. At times, 'Arnie's Army' would all run off to the next hole before you had even putted out. He was a great putter himself, despite all his antics and his huffing and puffing — some of that was a bit of an act.

He had this knock-kneed stance over the ball and was very wristy, but he was a helluva putter. He gave the impression that he was Superman, that he was totally fearless and completely in charge.

I remember playing with him and Jack Nicklaus that same year in the final round of the Canadian Open in Montreal. They were only televising the last three holes and on the tee at the 265-yard, par-4 16th there was one of those huge, old cameras slap bang in front of us.

Arnie was teeing his ball up, and Jack came up behind me and said, "Watch him when the camera's red light goes on."

Sure enough, Arnie started snorting like a bull at a matador. He looked up at his target like a TV tough guy, his shirt hanging out, and it looked like he was ready to shake the course by the scruff of the neck.

He struck his tee shot, gave the club a swashbuckling twirl at the end of his swing and the crowd was roaring. He was able to turn all that on for the cameras and the galleries, and, of course, the ball ended up in the middle of the green.

It was almost like watching John Wayne in a cowboy film. It was all about the delivery with Arnold. It was a special gift he possessed, and he used it to the best of his ability. Jack knew the format from their 'Big Three' TV days with Gary Player.

Neither Jack nor Gary could do that sort of thing because it just wasn't in them. Arnold was the first one to go out there and give the public the impression that he could shake every goddamn birdie he could out of the course and look tough while doing it.

He also had the backing of a great guy, a golf writer called Bob Drum. Like Arnold, Bob was from Pennsylvania, and he was central to building Palmer up to resemble a Greek God in those early days. They called him the 'King' for good reason back then.

It was typical of how America treated their stars. Palmer was a Gregory Peck, Cary Grant, Humphrey Bogart-type figure. They know how to take care of their special celebrities and Palmer certainly held a very privileged status in the game.

It was bloody difficult to play alongside him amid all the frenzy and the atmosphere. One of the greatest efforts in my playing career was to win the Jacksonville Open in Florida in March 1968.

In the final round, I was in the same group as Palmer and Don January, another prolific winner in the States, and winning that day under that sort of pressure proved a big stepping stone for me.

From that point on, I was aware I could deliver under intense pressure, and boosted by the confidence of knowing that I went on to win The Open in 1969 and the US Open in 1970.

I'd go as far as to say that between the spring of 1968 to early 1971, I don't think there was anyone better than me. South African Hugh Baiocchi said that if the world rankings had been around during that period, I would have been the number one.

I had to ignore all the hullabaloo around Palmer in that final round at Jacksonville. My first thought at the start of the day was, *"How the hell am I going to get through this?"*

It was a bit like going into the last round of a Major championship with a four-shot lead because you know if you don't win, you're going to get some stick, and all the pressure is on you.

I had also played in the 1966 World Cup with Palmer and by 1968, I realised I just had to focus fully on my own game. It was about taking the positives out of the situation. It was still a daunting task and to be able to win in Jacksonville, under those circumstances, was a massive deal for me.

It was the first win by a European on the PGA Tour since the 1920s and I couldn't have won The Open a year later without that experience behind me. When you play someone, who is better than you, and beat them, it does wonders for your psyche and self-belief.

Palmer didn't frighten me any more after Jacksonville. I just built up this armour of confidence around my game. There was no nastiness from his fans — if you hit a good shot, they would normally clap, just not as loudly as they did for him.

It was a bit like firefighting for me in those days. The less well-known players, especially in the UK — the likes of Dickinson, Bob Goalby and Dave Hill — made it clear that I wasn't welcome in America, and they wouldn't talk to me during rounds.

The best players — Palmer, Nicklaus, Lee Trevino and Johnny Miller — weren't like that at all. They welcomed me and just sort of said, "Come on, show us what you've got." It was the guys who never travelled overseas who had a chip on their shoulders.

A lot of them were very insular and they treated me very much like a foreigner. Those guys wanted to keep me out, as well as South African Harold Henning and the Australian pair Bruce Devlin and Bruce Crampton.

To be fair, those American guys were nice to me until I won. But they changed overnight because as far as they were concerned, I was invading their territory and they weren't happy about that.

I first travelled to America almost sixty years ago; I've lived there for almost thirty years, but I'll always feel like an outsider. To a lot of Americans, I'm still looked upon as 'That Limey'.

Chapter 3
1969 Matches

ROYAL BIRKDALE, SOUTHPORT, SEPTEMBER 18–20
Captains: E Brown (GB), S Snead (USA)
GREAT BRITAIN: 16, USA: 16

Foursomes: Morning
N Coles & B Huggett beat M Barber & R Floyd 3 & 2
B Gallacher & M Bembridge beat L Trevino & K Still 2 & 1
T Jacklin & P Townsend beat D Hill & T Aaron 3 & 1
C O'Connor & P Alliss halved with B Casper & F Beard

Foursomes: Afternoon
N Coles & B Huggett lost to D Hill & T Aaron by 1 hole
B Gallacher & M Bembridge lost to L Trevino & G Littler by 2 holes
T Jacklin & P Townsend beat B Casper & F Beard by 1 hole
P Butler & B Hunt lost to J Nicklaus & D Sikes by 1 hole

Fourballs: Morning
C O'Connor & P Townsend beat D Hill & D Douglass by 1 hole
B Huggett & G Caygill halved with R Floyd & M Barber
B Barnes & P Alliss lost to L Trevino & G Littler by 1 hole
T Jacklin & N Coles beat J Nicklaus & D Sikes by 1 hole

Fourballs: Afternoon:
P Butler & P Townsend lost to B Casper & F Beard by 2 holes
B Huggett & B Gallacher lost to D Hill & K Still 2 & 1
M Bembridge & B Hunt halved with T Aaron & R Floyd
T Jacklin & N Coles halved with L Trevino & M Barber

Singles: Morning

P Alliss lost to L Trevino 2 & 1

P Townsend lost to D Hill 5 & 4

N Coles beat T Aaron by 1 hole

B Barnes lost to B Casper by 1 hole

C O'Connor beat F Beard 5 & 4

M Bembridge beat K Still by 1 hole

P Butler beat R Floyd by 1 hole

T Jacklin beat J Nicklaus 4 & 3

Singles: Afternoon

B Barnes lost to D Hill 4 & 2

B Gallacher beat L Trevino 4 & 3

M Bembridge lost to M Barber 7 & 6

P Butler beat D Douglass 3 & 2

N Coles lost to D Sikes 4 & 3

C O'Connor lost to G Littler 2 & 1

B Huggett halved with B Casper

T Jacklin halved with J Nicklaus

Not in my wildest dreams could I imagine anyone else doing what Jack Nicklaus did in 1969.

The famous match-tying, last-hole concession at Royal Birkdale was a shock to me at the time. When he was standing over his 4½-footer at the last hole, I was leaning on my putter, saying to myself, "TJ, whatever happens, you are going to have to sink this one."

Jack converted his putt and I started to walk towards putting my ball down, but he already had my marker in his hand before I got there. He went on to tell me, "I don't think you'd have missed, but I wasn't going to give you the opportunity in these circumstances."

I truly never contemplated that happening. I think I'd have made my putt anyway. It was 20 to 24 inches long and I certainly hadn't missed anything of that length all week. But who the hell knows? Regardless, it was a wonderful way to end three days of excellent sportsmanship.

That one moment of remarkable generosity from Jack sits right up there as far as the history of our game is concerned. Golf separates itself from so many other sports in terms of honour and integrity.

If you can't look your opponent in the eye at the end of 18 holes and shake his hand whether you've won, lost or drawn, then we are all wasting our time.

That's definitely the spirit in which Jack and I played the game. His teammate Frank Beard said he would have made me putt. I knew Frank well, played a lot of golf with him and he was a tough guy. He was a "Give him that? Are you nuts?" kind of guy.

But Jack saw the bigger picture. He realised that Britain finally had a champion golfer, the first Open winner for eighteen years since Max Faulkner had triumphed at Royal Portrush.

Jack and I were good friends, and he didn't want to see anything happen that would spoil that, and he knew the Americans, as Cup holders, would've retained the trophy anyway.

He was able to think with clarity in very stressful circumstances; that was one of his great strengths. That was why he amassed a record eighteen Major victories. Jack had enjoyed a stellar amateur career as well and I think some of the lessons he learned at a very young age remained with him forever.

Neither of us believed the Ryder Cup was a war. We both wanted to beat each other but we wanted to win by outplaying our opponent when he was at his best.

A lot of Jack's values came from his days as an amateur. His father, who I had the privilege of playing with, instilled that in him. I remember reading somewhere about an incident in his much younger days when he was less than kind to an opponent and his father read him the riot act.

I always felt those standards stayed with him throughout his life. He didn't play the game like an amateur but in terms of what golf represents, his values are steeped in a lot of his amateur learnings.

We were interviewed about the 'Concession' a few years back and Jack's words summed up the man's caring human instincts. He said:

"What Tony had done in 1969 in winning the British Open, what it did for British golf, was something very special.

"The spirit of the Ryder Cup was as a goodwill match. If Tony would have missed that putt, I felt he would have been like a choking dog forever.

"I don't think he would have ever missed it but why would you ever want to give him the opportunity, when he has given Britain a hero and given them the opportunity to really cheer and root for somebody and put him up on a pedestal, to bring him down from that pedestal?

"If I had to do it again, I would do it again every single time."

As a celebration of that unforgettable sporting moment, Jack and I teamed up more than three decades later to build The Concession Golf Club in Florida.

It's been open since 2006 and is such a very special venue that perhaps, one day, it can be the proud setting for a Ryder Cup match. We created it in the hope that other people would come and enjoy the great game that has given the two of us so much pleasure for so long and to play golf in the same sort of spirit in which we did battle at Royal Birkdale all those years ago.

The fact of the matter is that I produced my finest ever Ryder Cup performance at Birkdale that week. My swing was just where I wanted it to be, and I was on top of the world due to my Open victory at Royal Lytham.

My biggest challenge when I first started playing in America in 1967 had been to slow my swing down. I was a good player back then, despite having a tendency to get too quick when I got excited, namely when I got into contention down the stretch in tournaments.

I needed to slow my upper body down and initiate the downward swing with my lower body while at the same time keeping my upper body slightly behind. It was important to let my legs get through the impact area flexed before following through with the rest of the body.

I recall a practice round I played with Ben Hogan in 1970 — soon after I'd won the US Open at Hazeltine — after he had politely turned me down at the 1967 Masters. I'd gone into the locker room with South African Bobby Cole and approached Hogan about going out together.

He was nice about it, but he said he had a lot of work to do before Thursday's start and that perhaps we could do it another time. The irony is that he approached me about playing together before the 1970 US PGA Championship in Tulsa, and it turned out to be the only time we shared 18 holes.

Hogan was just about IT as far as I was concerned. Nobody did it like he did. He was the best I ever saw in terms of control and ball striking. Everything he did was close to perfection. He had tremendous flex in his swing.

He used to talk a lot about the "Hogan Secret" and that was all about the way he fired the legs and the lower body towards the target just prior to finishing his backswing.

The double-jointed angle of his wrist gave him tremendous lag and he was able to take the club all the way back before letting his legs fire and accentuating that natural flex.

There was such forward momentum coming from his lower body and the flex and lag he had meant that he was able to get through the ball on the target line much more than most.

There's a funny story attached to that incident in Tulsa. While we were on the practice green, a Texas pro by the name of Terry Dill came up to me and asked if he could join Hogan, Jackie Burke and me.

"Hey Tony," he enquired, "y'all have a game?"

I went up to Hogan to ask if it was OK for Terry to join us, but he said "no".

I walked back to Terry and said, "Sorry, Terry, it looks like we're all set."

Then, five holes later, we were in sight of the first tee, and Terry was still there on the practice green. I felt terrible that he could see we were only a three and there would have been room for him to join us.

Hogan came up to me and announced that Terry had approached him before. "Do you know what he said to me?" Hogan muttered, "he asked me how I prepared for Major championships. I replied that the first thing I do is never talk to other people in practice!"

Hogan took no prisoners, but he was always very good to me, very polite. I don't think anybody in my lifetime in golf was held in as high a regard. He was revered for his dedication and work ethic.

Hogan, Nicklaus, Cary Middlecoff, Byron Nelson and Tommy Bolt were all great examples of a flexed lower body and flexed knees on the downswing. My two great friends on the PGA Tour, Tom Weiskopf and Bert Yancey, were the same because they never straightened their knees either.

Bolt had mentored Weiskopf, who developed a beautiful swing. I could never learn to recreate that flexed lower body action in the UK. Few new courses were being built at home and even when they were, they were made on a shoestring budget.

Between 1963 and 1967 I played mainly on links courses. You were always compromised by the weather there and it was tough to work on technique in those conditions.

Some courses didn't even have practice facilities in those days and therefore you often couldn't warm up before a round — you would just get out of your car and go straight to the first tee.

For me, Hogan was to golf the way Rudolf Nureyev was to ballet. His swing was so stylish, so classical and it never changed.

I hit thousands of balls in America in 1967, 1968 and 1969 with my seven-iron. It was my transition club where I needed a full swing without having to muscle the ball, and it helped me perfect the leg action I needed to compete with the world's best players.

Everyone in the 1960s and 1970s hit the seven-iron 150 yards and the great irony was that was the shot I had to hit into the last green when I won The Open at Lytham.

I was 145 yards away and I said to myself, "Hell, this is the shot I've been practising for the last three years."

It was such an important club for me and once I got my tempo right, I had total confidence I could harness all the power in my swing and compete at the highest level — I didn't have that at the 1967 Ryder Cup, but I sure had it two years later at Birkdale.

My win at Lytham took a helluva lot out of me. I wanted to go away and contemplate the enormity of my achievement for a few weeks, but my manager, Mark McCormack, insisted I pack my bags for America. I was wiped out, though.

It was the worst thing I could have done, and I missed four cuts in a row. If you want to play winning golf, you need to have your body and mind ready for action at the same time and I was a long way from being in that state.

It took me until the Ryder Cup to get my breath back and get everything where it needed to be. If you are mentally stressed you have to take a timeout, but by September I had my game and my desire back.

The US team was full of rookies — ten of them in fact. Our side was a good blend of youth and experience and we all got on well too. It was the first Ryder Cup for the Scot Bernard Gallacher and the two Englishmen, Peter Townsend and Maurice Bembridge.

Alex Caygill was playing in his one and only Ryder Cup. I used to think he and I were great friends. The two of us travelled together a lot but when I shot a remarkable 29 on the front nine in The Open at St Andrews in 1970 before the heavens opened and rain stopped play, all he kept saying was, "Lucky bugger, lucky bugger, lucky bugger."

Who would say that to a guy who had won the championship a year earlier and started off like a runaway train in the first round a year later? That episode, I'm afraid, ended any friendship we had.

I partnered Townsend in my first two 1969 Ryder Cup matches. He and I had played boys' golf together and his first wife Lorna and my first wife Vivien were good friends. He won his playing privileges in America at the same time as me and we spent a lot of downtime going out as a foursome in the evening.

Townsend was one of my best friends. Simple as that. We won both matches but, inexplicably, we were split up on the second day. Eric Brown was our captain, and he didn't tell us why.

I teamed up with Neil Coles on the Friday and we picked up 1½ points from our two games. Neil and I also got on well. He was a terrific player; a particularly good putter and he minded his own business.

But the way Townsend and I were split up was typical of how amateurish our side was back then. We were always flying by the seat of our pants. Even the rules officials were off the pace and people often forget what a small operation the competition was in those days.

Townsend didn't achieve much in playing terms in America. But to attempt to go out there in 1967, 1968, you had to be one of the top players in Britain and he was. He certainly could play; his drawback was that he developed a mystery shot.

He never knew when it would pop up but when it did the ball went sideways. But he was a winner at home and a great young player as a boy. He was half the size of most guys, but Brown would have looked at him as one of the strengths of the team.

It was a bit of a watershed year for British golf in 1969. I won The Open and we tied the Ryder Cup 16-16 to end a long sequence of American dominance. Our performances that year gave the game a shot in the arm and injected a lot of enthusiasm into the crowds.

Townsend and I beat Dave Hill and Tommy Aaron 3 & 1 in the morning foursomes. Hill was a bit crazy, always ready for an argument, but a good player too.

It all kicked off on the second afternoon when Hill and Ken Still took on Gallacher and Brian Huggett. Hill putted up to 12 inches before proceeding to tap his ball in, but Gallacher said, "You can't do that. This is match-play golf and the furthest from the hole always plays first."

Hill retorted: "If you want to play like that, we'll give you the hole."

The two pairs really went at it and there was plenty of bad blood between them. Still was a good guy, I liked him, but he was a bit highly strung and liked to shout and scream.

Two matches behind, Coles and I were playing against Lee Trevino and Miller Barber. It was a helluva challenge getting through both sessions before the light faded, especially as the morning fourballs took a particularly long time.

It was already getting dark on the 16th, never mind the 18th. The match went down to the wire and the officials arranged for a load of drivers to put their car headlights on near the clubhouse so we could finish.

It was insane. We all messed up because of course you can't putt if you can't see, but all's well that ends well because Coles and I picked up a half-point.

The Daily Express was giving away a Tony Jacklin putter housed in a case for the week's best performer and, lo and behold, it went to me! I picked up five points from my six matches and the two teams celebrated the tie in style at the end.

I had played Nicklaus twice in the last-day singles, beating him 4 & 3 in the morning before our unforgettable halved match later on.

I bogeyed the 16th in the afternoon to go one down before holing a ridiculous putt from 50 feet right across the green for an outrageous eagle at the 17th. A massive roar went up and at the same time in the match ahead, Huggett had a 4½-footer at the last against Billy Casper.

Huggett mistakenly thought the roars had signalled another point for me against Nicklaus and when he knocked in his putt, he thought overall victory was ours. He broke down, wetting Brown's jacket lapels with his tears, and the captain had to break the news that my putt on 17 was to get back to all square, not for a win.

The whole thing typified how tenacious a player Huggett was. He was a tough little blighter on the golf course, a good putter, and there was never any quitting from him.

Brown strolled back down the fairway towards Nicklaus and me. We'd hit our tee shots, both three-woods. The captain asked in his heavy Scottish brogue, "You know what you've gotta do?"

I replied, "Yes, Eric, I know what I've gotta do."

I had walked on ahead of Nicklaus, but he hollered after me. "Tony?' he called out. I waited until he caught up. "I just wanted to ask you something," he continued, "are you nervous?"

I replied that I was petrified. "If it's any consolation," he said, "I feel the same way."

The other twenty players were all around the green and that's when you realise the pressure surrounding the Ryder Cup beats everything else in golf because it's not just yourself you're playing for, it's the entire team; the country too.

The spirit in my match with Nicklaus was pure. It was fantastic to be a part of. Another grand gesture people tend to forget was that the PGA of America allowed us to have the trophy in 1970, which they didn't have to do as holders.

I don't think that had ever been done before and they would have been well within their rights to have it for each of the two years before the next edition in 1971.

Things like that, the great sportsmanship from Nicklaus, helped to enhance the Ryder Cup. It's never been warfare as far as I'm concerned. I was involved in seven matches as a player and four as captain and the only time I've been concerned about the atmosphere was in 1991.

Things went too far that year with all the 'War by the Shore' stuff and the Desert Storm caps for some of the US the players. It was treading dangerous ground but there was nothing like that in 1969.

It was a grand celebration, both teams had a good party at the end, and everyone was happy. Sadly, for the Great Britain team, it would be a long time before we partied again because we slipped back into our old ways throughout the 1970s and were well beaten time and again.

To be fair, there had been some antagonism at Birkdale. Brown and US captain Sam Snead both had tough-guy reputations. Our skipper was a fiery Scot and had been involved in numerous run-ins with other players in his career.

Snead was the same. He was a country boy from Virginia who simply didn't give a damn. He knew his legendary status in the game — having won a record 82 PGA Tour titles, including seven Majors — and for the press, his battle for supremacy with Brown was a match made in heaven.

The Hill-Still thing added a bit of extra spice but, beyond that, there was no real conflict. In those days, the relationship between both teams was not as cordial as it has become in recent decades.

There wasn't the mutual respect that is evident now. It was a different era. The players didn't go out of their way to be pleasant but, equally, there were no fisticuffs. The atmosphere was more tense than it would be today.

Brown did tell us not to look for any balls if the Americans found the rough, but the players took no notice. That's a load of bull. I didn't want to win that way. I wanted my opponent to be in top form when I won, and I couldn't have lived with myself if I saw a ball in the rough and didn't help.

That comment from Brown was a dream for the press, you can imagine the headlines it caused. Snead also said his team hadn't come over to be "good 'ole boys"; it was all about winning for him.

Despite all the alleged protestations about the famous concession, Nicklaus assures me Snead never said a damned thing to him at the end.

Snead was in his pomp as a player in the 1950s, when it was hard going, a lot of rough and tumble. Those guys had to fight for everything. There was no air-conditioning, they had to drive from town to town from one week to the next, wives in tow. It wasn't as easy as it has become today, and they had to develop a thick skin.

They were selfish, they had to be, and you didn't go out of your way to make pleasant conversations with your playing partner. Attitudes were different and, thank God, it's changed for the better.

When I went over to the States and befriended Weiskopf and Yancey, we would pull for each other, practice together, help each other. If we saw anything we'd say something but go back 15 years before that and the players certainly wouldn't have been sharing their secrets.

Do you think Hogan would share secrets? He'd keep it all to himself. It's different today; everyone is comfortable financially; they all travel first class, stay in the best hotel suites each week.

In the Sixties, we used to stay in bog-standard motels. In fact, when I started out, I couldn't even afford to stay in those. I'd write ahead of the tournaments to club members or people attached to the venues where we planned to play to ask if I could stay with them.

Trevino, of course, was one of the American Ryder Cup rookies at Birkdale. He and I played a lot of golf together in that era, and he was just as talkative in 1969 as he was later in his career.

He was a helluva player, but he used that incessant chatter on the course as part of his arsenal. It seemed to calm him down and, as an opponent, you had to endure it.

There was an occasion in the World Match Play Championship at Wentworth when I was four down on the first hole of the second 18 and he's going at it hammer and tongs. I turned around and said, "Look, Lee, I don't want to talk; I just want to play."

He replied, "That's OK, you don't have to talk, just listen."

You never had to deal with that from anyone else. Palmer, Nicklaus would say 'good shot', 'bad shot', this and that but Trevino would even talk away on his backswing. It would gee him up; it was all about him, no one else.

There might even have been an element of mind games in it, gamesmanship. For some people, it was putting something in their heads just before they hit the ball.

I experienced that quite a bit in America with the likes of Dan Sikes, who also played at Birkdale in 1969, Hill, Bob Goalby and Gardner Dickinson. They were not very nice at all.

I played with Sikes at Doral one year. I was leading going down the ninth, an island hole, in the final round and he turned around and said, "I played with Tommy Aaron here last year. He was also leading, and he put his ball in the water."

Sure enough, my ball ended up wet too.

I found Sikes horrible and anti-visitors, though he went on to become a key player in the formation of today's PGA Tour.

Hill would say any goddamn thing. He was off the charts. You looked into his eyes, and his pupils were so small. He was an angry man and prided himself on being unfriendly. His brother Mike had a fantastic senior career.

They were a tough pair and you met plenty more in America with that sort of approach than you did in Britain, where people tended to get along more.

Ours is a tightly packed island, so you have to get on with your neighbour. Europe is on our doorstep and travel is the greatest university there is. I certainly didn't learn much at school. I left at fifteen, and the world was my education, travelling, playing golf, playing with presidents, kings. It was a fantastic schooling.

In 1969, I was where I needed to be, very strong mentally, and I was determined. Underlying all of my effort was the desire I had to be the best player in the world, and I knew I had to beat Nicklaus and the like to achieve that.

I never told myself I was the best player but something my dad told me as a teenager struck a chord. He said, "Tone, you know they've only got two arms, two legs and one head — just the same as you — so don't treat them any differently to you." That sentiment has always stayed with me.

Away from the course, I was a bit of a joker who had lots of laughs, but golf was a serious business as soon as I stepped on that first tee. Playing in the US hardened me, especially seeing how some of the Americans treated me.

I knew I'd have to adopt an attitude of my own to give no quarter on the course. That didn't mean I wanted to win by default; I just didn't want to be guilty of not trying enough to get what I desperately wanted.

Chapter 4
1971 Matches

OLD WARSON COUNTRY CLUB, ST LOUIS, MISSOURI,
SEPTEMBER 16–18
Captains: E Brown (GB), J Hebert (USA)
GREAT BRITAIN: 13½, USA: 18½

Foursomes: Morning

N Coles & C O'Connor beat B Casper & M Barber 2 & 1

P Townsend & P Oosterhuis lost to A Palmer & G Dickinson by 2 holes

B Huggett & T Jacklin beat J Nicklaus & D Stockton 3 & 2

M Bembridge & P Butler beat C Coody & F Beard by 1 hole

Foursomes: Afternoon

H Bannerman & B Gallacher beat B Casper & M Barber 2 & 1

P Townsend & P Oosterhuis lost to A Palmer & G Dickinson by 1 hole

B Huggett & T Jacklin halved with L Trevino & M Rudolph

M Bembridge & P Butler lost to J Nicklaus & JC Snead 5 & 3

Fourballs: Morning

C O'Connor & B Barnes lost to L Trevino & M Rudolph 2 & 1

N Coles & J Garner lost to F Beard & JC Snead 2 & 1

P Oosterhuis & B Gallacher lost to A Palmer & G Dickinson 5 & 4

P Townsend & H Bannerman lost to J Nicklaus & G Littler 2 & 1

Fourballs: Afternoon

B Gallacher & P Oosterhuis beat L Trevino & B Casper by 1 hole

T Jacklin & B Huggett lost to G Littler & JC Snead 2 & 1

P Townsend & H Bannerman lost to A Palmer & J Nicklaus by 1 hole
N Coles & C O'Connor halved with C Coody & F Beard

Singles: Morning
T Jacklin lost to L Trevino by 1 hole
B Gallacher halved with D Stockton
B Barnes beat M Rudolph 1 hole
P Oosterhuis beat G Littler 4 & 3
P Townsend lost to J Nicklaus 3 & 2
C O'Connor lost to G Dickinson 5 & 4
H Bannerman halved with A Palmer
N Coles halved with F Beard

Singles: Afternoon
B Huggett lost to L Trevino 7 & 6
T Jacklin lost to JC Snead by 1 hole
B Barnes beat M Barber 2 & 1
P Townsend lost to D Stockton by 1 hole
B Gallacher beat C Coody 2 & 1
N Coles lost to J Nicklaus 5 & 3
P Oosterhuis beat A Palmer 3 & 2
H Bannerman beat G Dickinson 2 & 1

I got a bit of a bollocking shortly after arriving in America for the 1971 Ryder Cup and it proved the launch pad to a less than satisfying week.

The Great Britain team touched down in St Louis and, following my two Major victories in 1969 and 1970, the media had only one man in their sights because nobody over there would have recognised our Scottish captain Eric Brown.

As soon as we landed, I was surrounded by the media and I kept saying, "I'm just one player in our team, the captain's over there, go and talk to HIM."

I might just as well have been speaking Swahili because they continued swarming around me. I was talking, talking, talking — giving loads of interviews — and suddenly a guy turned up at the airport with a beautiful Rolls-Royce and offered me a lift to the team hotel.

By the time I'd finished a seemingly never-ending round of interviews, the team bus was jam-packed. Some people were standing in the aisles with their luggage so I asked British PGA secretary John Bywaters if I could take the Rolls-Royce and he said "yes".

When we got to the hotel, Brown came up and asked to speak to me. He said in his heavy Scottish brogue, "I dinnae want to see you travelling in Rolls-Royces while the rest of us are riding in a bus."

My reply was, "Fair-dos Eric, no problem, but the bus was crammed, and I did ask John for permission."

That was the end of the episode. I took the bollocking on the chin and no one else said a word about it. I was the main man at the time, our number one player, and I guess everyone was aware of that.

That was the fact of the matter and I'd like to think there was no arrogance or anything like that on my part. It was a circumstantial thing, there was no lingering animosity from anyone.

As usual, we got our arses kicked that week. It wasn't for want of trying; I gave it my all, but I didn't play well. If truth be told, it wasn't a great year for me. I'd won the very first Lancôme Trophy in France late in 1970 but my form wasn't up to much the following year.

I was going through a lot of stuff away from golf. Vivien and I upped sticks and moved from Lincolnshire to Gloucestershire in order to be closer to London for easier access to air travel. My son Bradley had not long been born and we also had Warren on the way too.

It's probably fair to say my golf took a bit of a nosedive in 1971. I was doing the same things to prepare, putting in the same amount of time, but you've got to turn up at tournaments with mind and body as one and you can't always be on top form, for whatever reason.

I did, though, have a very good week at The Open. I would have finished second behind my old nemesis, Lee Trevino, but for a freak incident on the last hole.

Taiwan's Lu Liang Huan, who played in a distinctive pork-pie hat and was known by everyone as 'Mr Lu', struck a woman on the head with a wild second shot and left her partially concussed.

The woman was standing in the rough and, after the ball had very fortunately deflected out into the middle of the fairway, she apparently told Mr Lu to "go and get another birdie for me". He then had an easy pitch on to the green before holing his birdie putt to clinch second place, one stroke ahead of me.

In truth, I struggled to perform at my best all week. My long game was all over the place, but I was rescued by a fantastic touch on the greens — I barely missed a putt inside eight feet.

I felt so bad about my game from tee-to-green that I had a session with the renowned swing coach John Jacobs in the middle of the tournament.

A perfect tempo was always central for me to be at my best, and it was off that week.

More than anything, a good tempo improves the quality of your bad shots if you're thrashing it around. I was always a good driver of the ball and everything else in my game used to just fall into place if that element was secure, but I was erratic off the tee at Royal Birkdale and when that happened, I used to start second-guessing myself and my confidence was affected.

Such was the excellence of my putting that I was in contention all week. I shared the lead on 69 with Trevino, Argentina's Vicente Fernandez and American Howie Johnson after the first round.

Johnson was in the same bracket as Bob Goalby, Gardner Dickinson and Dave Hill. I remember after I won the US Open, he turned around and said, "Goddamn it, you holed some putts last week."

I replied, "What's wrong with saying 'well played' when you win a Major championship by seven strokes?" But he wasn't capable of saying that sort of thing.

Trevino and I were joint leaders after the second round at Birkdale and I trailed the man affectionately known as 'Supermex' by a solitary stroke after the third — prompting one memorable newspaper headline: *It's Lee and Lu and you know who!*

I was sniffing around all week, mainly because everyone else was missing short putts. Links courses were right up Trevino's street, and his game was made for them. He was a straight hitter and a good putter.

The greens were spongy, full of thatch, and were so bad that they had to be dug up soon after. I got away with it that week solely because of a hot putter.

The prize money was pathetic. Trevino won £5,500 and I picked up £3,250. I think I was born at the wrong time when you see the millions swilling around for the modern-day players.

I bought a Rolls-Royce for £10,000 in 1971, Mediterranean blue with a white interior, and it looked spectacular. I have blown quite a bit of money on cars in my time. I also purchased a Jensen Interceptor at one point but went on to wreck it around 1971, 1972.

Sometime before that, I had bought an Aston Martin DB5, one of the first made. I took it back to the factory in Newport Pagnell and spent £200 getting it in pristine shape.

When I went to pick it up, the James Bond Aston Martin that Sean Connery drove in the films was sat there gathering dust, the one with the shield at the back to stop the bullets penetrating the windows.

I eventually sold my version for £1,375 and I read recently that it would have been worth $4 million today. That seems a barely believable thought to contemplate!

The fact of the matter is there was no money in vintage cars in the early Seventies but, when that changed, the Bond car sold at auction for $6 million. It just goes to prove that timing is everything in life.

The Jenson Interceptor was a four-wheel drive and, accustomed as I was to driving the Aston Martin, it tended to drift, and it was a bit like driving on railway tracks.

I was in Lincolnshire once with Peter Townsend, took a corner too quickly, skidded on some gravel and ended up in a ditch. We were okay but it was a shame about the car because it was lilac. The manufacturers made it especially because the sweater I wore in the final round at the 1969 Open was that colour.

Anyhow, back to the Ryder Cup in St Louis. At around this time, I thought the Americans were influencing the format of four fourballs, four foursomes, and two singles sessions. They always wanted to triumph at all costs and if they thought they could win every one of the matches, that would have suited them just fine.

It wasn't until 1981 that we managed to set in stone the schedule of four fourballs, four foursomes and one singles session that we still use today.

The old format was a big advantage for the Americans because it was not so easy for us to hide our weaker players. The schedule we use now is perfect because it produces a close finish to the matches nine times out of ten — and that's what we need to maintain long-term interest.

We were still feeling very inferior in 1971, travelling second-class at the back of the bus as usual. There were still no team rooms and Eric Brown pretty much left us to our own devices.

The cigar-smoking Scot, Harry Bannerman, made his debut that year. He was a good guy, and I enjoyed his company. We went out shopping one day and he bought a flash red jacket that he couldn't resist.

We had some colourful characters in our team in St Louis: Harry, Brian Barnes and Christy O'Connor Senior. It was also Peter Oosterhuis' debut, and my fellow Englishman was a fine player.

The media tried to create a rivalry between Oosty and me in the 1970s, but the truth is that we got on really well. We were good friends, and the talk of animosity was a load of baloney.

We played each other in the World Match Play Championship at Wentworth one year. I thought it was important to beat him at that time in our individual careers, but I always enjoyed Oosty's company. He was a good putter and very competitive in Ryder Cups.

I played a part in him getting into TV commentary. I used to do quite a bit of that but became tired of it and I recommended him to Sky Sports.

I told them to give Oosty a shot; one thing led to another, and he ended up becoming a regular.

It's extremely sad that he's now suffering from Alzheimer's. He's had a rough time in recent years. The two of us have always got on so well and I like him a lot.

Thinking of our so-called rivalry, it makes me recall the one that started to develop between Nick Faldo and Sandy Lyle at the 1980 Kenya Open.

Lyle put some tape over his putter to stop the sun's glare bouncing off it. Faldo informed the authorities and it ended up with his Ryder Cup teammate being disqualified.

From my point of view, it was fair dos because if sticking tape on your putter is not allowed, that's the end of the story. I know that incident changed Lyle's view of Faldo, but they were always okay in the team room when I went on to become captain.

Faldo never took any prisoners. He was always all about himself, totally self-centred, and that's how you've got to be when you are yearning to be the number-one player on the planet.

He didn't care about having friends. He is more amenable in the commentary box these days but, as a player, he was completely engrossed in his own game. He was an only son, doted on by his mum and nothing else mattered to him other than winning golf tournaments.

He wouldn't have cared less what Lyle thought about him in Kenya, but I can tell you I've been in their company many times since that incident, and they get on now and have a laugh together.

They are big boys and there's no animosity any more. They have great respect for one another's achievements, and they've moved on.

As big-name players and multiple Major winners, Faldo and Lyle never felt overwhelmed by the thought of taking on the Americans in the Ryder Cup every couple of years.

That certainly wasn't the case for the majority of our players in the Sixties and Seventies. We were doing everything on a shoestring budget, and it told on us. It affected our collective psyche, and our self-esteem was injured.

As a twice Major winner and a regular on the US PGA Tour, I was well entrenched in the American way in 1971 but some of our guys were overwhelmed by it, even though they would never admit it.

The local media called the Americans 'The Super Team'. They had Palmer, Nicklaus, Trevino and Casper, another multiple Major champion. Arnold, Jack and Lee won 13 points in St Louis — they effectively beat our team on their own.

And I recall their captain, Jay Hebert, celebrating in style at the end. He was a real character, but he found it a struggle to string two coherent words together at the closing ceremony.

Hebert had obviously downed a drink or five and was definitely three sheets to the wind by the end of the day, totally gone.

There were no inhibitions in the American camp in those days, and it's much the same for our modern-day Europeans too. They're all fired up and totally up for it now because virtually all of them play regularly in the States and there is no longer a fear factor involved.

They've always had big names in the US team; there's generally a legend or two in their side, absolute megastars. Hollywood was partly responsible for their super swagger in my days as a player.

Hollywood represented Americans as invincible, so the players had a legacy to lean on, which was a massive advantage.

That was the history, and it was very real. No disrespect to Brian Waites but when a humble club professional from Notts Golf Club tees it up against an American superstar — as he did under my captaincy in 1983 — it's going to be intimidating for him.

I mentioned my supposed rivalry with Oosterhuis earlier, and the real antagonism between Faldo and Lyle, but Palmer and Nicklaus played together in the 1971 Ryder Cup and there was not the slightest hint of ego getting in their way.

The two of them had played together several times in team events; I'd played against them at the 1966 World Cup in Japan. Palmer and Nicklaus got on well and were friends.

They had played so much televised 'Big Three' golf together all over the world with Gary Player and were completely at ease in each other's company.

We actually made a good start to the 1971 Ryder Cup, going 3-1 up after the opening foursomes. Brian Huggett and I teamed up to defeat Nicklaus and Dave Stockton 3 & 2 and we also paired up in the afternoon to take a half-point against Trevino and Mason Rudolph after I chipped in at the last hole.

That was the last meaningful contribution I was to make that week. I missed the second day fourballs and then Huggett and I lost 2 & 1 to Gene Littler and JC Snead in the afternoon foursomes.

There were two singles sessions on the final day, and I was beaten one up by Trevino and then again by the same margin by Snead.

Oosterhuis enjoyed a terrific debut, picking up three points, while Bernard Gallacher did even better by notching three and a half.

Gallacher was a terrific battler in the Ryder Cup. He was an up-and-at-em type of player, tough to beat, a superb putter and he squeezed the absolute maximum out of his talents.

He wasn't a good driver of the ball; he hit it out of the neck of the club at times, but my, oh, my, what a fighter he was. The two of us were close; our wives were close and the pair of us were always really into the Ryder Cup.

However, Gallacher was involved in one almighty cock-up in 1971 when he and Oosty were up against Palmer and Dickinson in the morning fourballs on the second day.

Palmer delivered a sumptuous tee shot with his five-iron at the par-three seventh that finished pin high. Then, as Gallacher walked on to the tee with his three-iron, his caddie asked Arnold's bagman what club they had used.

That, of course, is not allowed. It is deemed a contravention of the rules, an illegal request for advice, and the referee immediately awarded the hole to the Americans.

Gallacher was a great ally in all four of my matches as captain, once as a player and the rest as my chief off-course lieutenant. He and I never started a match believing we were one down before we'd even begun, but I'm not sure I can say the same for some of the others.

As I mentioned earlier, there's a massive difference between bravado and confidence — two totally different animals. If you're a professional golfer, you have to think, "I'm gonna beat this bugger, I can do this," even though in your heart of hearts, you may be fearful.

Looking back, I find it very difficult to put it into words but some of our guys were very British in attitude and to a lot of the American players they appeared aloof and standoffish.

Sam Snead never took to the great Sir Henry Cotton, for example, because he was typically British. The likes of John Jacobs and Bernard Hunt were in the same mould. They were reserved, not very outgoing, and wouldn't be rubbing shoulders with the Americans, telling jokes or generally trying to engender any warmth.

I always had the feeling that for some of our team, it was about turning up and being good sports rather than actually winning. The Americans had all the right gear; they looked the part, dressed in dapper style — everything they had was better than what we had.

It was tough for anyone who hadn't played in America to understand what it's like to play over there. To the locals, the Americans are the only ones that matter.

You see that attitude on the Seniors Tour at the moment. Bernhard Langer is breaking record after record, but Fred Couples gets all the lucrative off-the-course deals, and, at the end of the day, he'll be worth millions more.

The Ryder Cup was so one-sided in my days as a player that the whole competition was on the verge of dying.

If our success hadn't come in the 1980s, there would be no Presidents Cup now, no Solheim Cup for the women.

People like Greg Norman and Gary Player picked up on the popularity of the Ryder Cup, they saw this amazing camaraderie the matches engendered, the shows of emotion, and they wanted some of that too because being Australian and South African meant that participating in the biennial event was never an option for them.

Everything in team golf followed as a result of the success we achieved – a lot of people forget that. The Americans still have a massive advantage in the Presidents Cup because of the format and the fact that the International Team don't possess the same depth.

The Internationals have only won once before, in 1998 at Royal Melbourne. I'll never forget what happened that year. I was licking my chops in anticipation of sitting in front of the TV to watch how it would all unfold on the final day and, suddenly, ESPN pulled the plug on their TV coverage.

That tells you everything you need to know. The Americans never want to be seen losing. From a ratings point of view, they need to see their own team winning.

In women's golf, Europe's Solheim team are now treated the same as their US counterparts and that's the reason we get magical finishes to the event like the one we witnessed in 2019.

Suzann Pettersen's performance at Gleneagles was truly phenomenal. It was a story for the ages, but the truth is, these competitions would not have ignited if we hadn't lit the blue touch paper in the Ryder Cup in the Eighties.

My attitude was that anyone can beat anyone in match play golf. It's so different to stroke play. It doesn't matter if you're Ben Hogan, Tiger Woods, Jack Nicklaus — you are there to be shot at.

For instance, I would back Player to beat Nicklaus every day of the week in match play because of his great short game. That aspect of match play golf is often overlooked.

Some American journalists were left with red faces after the European victory in Paris in 2018. 'Who can possibly beat our powerhouses Brooks Koepka or Dustin Johnson,' they were saying.

But match play is a different animal and team unity is a crucial ingredient too. Being together as much as possible on and off the course plays a huge role.

We got our backsides kicked again in 1971, losing by 18½ points to 13½. But Gallacher was an example of someone who totally got it. I remember he was playing with his fellow Scot Bannerman against Casper and Miller Barber.

"If we cannae beat these two guys we need to chuck it in," Gallacher told his partner with the American pair in close attendance. Casper and Barber were no slouches but it's the mentality that is so important.

Bravado is no substitute for confidence and Gallacher's up-and-at-'em style was just what was needed.

Chapter 5
1973 Matches

MUIRFIELD, SCOTLAND, SEPTEMBER 20–22
Captains: B Hunt (GB & Ireland), J Burke (USA)
GREAT BRITAIN & IRELAND: 13, USA: 19

Foursomes: Morning

B Barnes & B Gallacher beat L Trevino & B Casper by 1 hole

C O'Connor & N Coles beat T Weiskopf & JC Snead 3 & 2

T Jacklin & P Oosterhuis halved with J Rodriguez & L Graham

M Bembridge & E Polland lost to J Nicklaus & A Palmer 6 & 5

Fourballs: Afternoon

B Barnes & B Gallacher beat T Aaron & G Brewer 5 & 4

M Bembridge & B Huggett beat A Palmer & J Nicklaus 3 & 1

T Jacklin & P Oosterhuis beat T Weiskopf & B Casper 3 & 1

C O'Connor & N Coles lost to L Trevino & H Blancas 2 & 1

Foursomes: Morning

B Barnes & P Butler lost to J Nicklaus & T Weiskopf by 1 hole

T Jacklin & P Oosterhuis beat A Palmer & D Hill by 2 holes

M Bembridge & B Huggett beat J Rodriguez & L Graham 5 & 4

N Coles & C O'Connor lost to L Trevino & B Casper 2 & 1

Fourballs: Afternoon

B Barnes & P Butler lost to JC Snead & A Palmer by 2 holes

T Jacklin & P Oosterhuis lost to G Brewer & B Casper 3 & 2

C Clark & E Polland lost to J Nicklaus & T Weiskopf 3 & 2

M Bembridge & B Huggett halved with L Trevino & H Blancas

Singles: Morning

B Barnes lost to B Casper 2 & 1

B Gallacher lost to T Weiskopf 3 & 1

P Butler lost to H Blancas 5 & 4

T Jacklin beat T Aaron 2 & 1

N Coles halved with G Brewer

C O'Connor lost to JC Snead by 1 hole

M Bembridge halved with J Nicklaus

P Oosterhuis halved with L Trevino

Singles: Afternoon

B Huggett beat H Blancas 4 & 2

B Barnes lost to JC Snead 3 & 1

B Gallacher lost to G Brewer 6 & 5

T Jacklin lost to B Casper 2 & 1

N Coles lost to L Trevino 6 & 5

C O'Connor halved with T Weiskopf

M Bembridge lost to J Nicklaus by 2 holes

P Oosterhuis beat A Palmer 4 & 2

Forget the golf. Far more significant than the matches against the Americans was the car crash my father was involved in before the final day at Muirfield.

In that Ryder Cup encounter, there were eight singles in the morning and another eight in the afternoon. I started off by beating US Masters champion Tommy Aaron 2 & 1 but then lost by the same margin to Billy Casper.

No one wanted to upset me, so they kept my father's accident a secret until the end of play. Some officials came up to inform me as soon as I'd finished against Casper, and it was a terrible shock.

My dad was fifty-five or fifty-six at the time, and the steering wheel of his car had broken his jaw and knocked his teeth out. He had to stay in hospital for several days and drink soup from a straw for at least two months.

I wanted to go straight to the hospital after the matches but my manager, the American Mark McCormack, insisted I had to fulfil an obligation to fly to Switzerland for a pro-am event run by Bruce Rappaport, who owned the Inter Maritime shipping company.

The pair of us had a blazing row after I said I would have to pull out of the pro-am. Rappaport was at Muirfield too, and I don't know if it was to try and show a bit of muscle in front of him, but McCormack made a big issue of it and said I had to honour my commitments.

At one point, McCormack called me "a son of a bitch". I turned around and told him, "I'm no son of a bitch... I'm just doing what any normal son would do in the same circumstances."

Rappaport himself seemed fine about it all but my relationship with McCormack went rapidly downhill. It proved a key moment because I never got any attention from him after that.

He was busy doing other things while I was being pushed from pillar to post by other members of his International Management Group. I did the right thing by sticking to my guns and going to see my dad.

The exhibition get-together in Switzerland was a lucrative event. IMG would send Rappaport a list of players with different fees next to their names and he would tick off who he wanted.

Everything at the pro-am was first class. Rappaport was very rich and when you went to his house, you were served Chateau Lafite Rothschild, one of the world's most expensive wines.

He was a nice guy. I saw him years later, around 1989 or 1990, during a tournament at Gleneagles and he had a bottle of champagne delivered to the table I was sharing with my wife, Astrid.

Hearing about the car crash was a dreadful moment. Dad and I were best pals; he was an avid golfer and had been there for all the big occasions in my career.

Dad went to the Masters at Augusta National with me in 1969 and also travelled down to Australia to watch me play at the end of that year.

He was a golf nut. It was a great adventure for him, and he got to know a lot of the players.

My eldest son Bradley was born in November 1969, so Vivien couldn't travel. The sponsors Down Under gave me two air tickets and, rather than pass up on one of them, I decided to take Dad.

I finished fourth in the Australian Dunlop at Royal Sydney behind the winner Bruce Devlin, Lee Trevino and Gary Player but didn't fare so well in Yarra Yarra, where two closing 77s meant I ended up in 35th place at the Australian Open.

Vivien's parents had by then escaped from the political troubles in Northern Ireland by emigrating to St Kilda, a beachside suburb of Melbourne, and my dad and I took the chance to visit them, too.

We also took in a stop to Las Vegas for a golf tournament. But my dad was a creature of habit and flying through so many time zones had a sizeable impact on his body clock.

He found that part of it all a bit of a struggle and when we landed back in England, he shook my hand and said, "Tone, thank you for a great time but don't ask me again."

When McCormack insisted it was more important for me to go to Switzerland for a pro-am for $10,000, there was no contest. I was never going to do that instead of visiting my sick dad in hospital.

Dad was tremendously proud of my golfing achievements. He saw it all from the beginning, right back to when I took on and beat all the local professionals over two rounds to win the Lincolnshire Open as a sixteen-year-old.

I remember vividly when I got my first handicap in the summer of 1957 at the age of thirteen. Club members in those days wanted to keep the juniors out, but they couldn't stop us going in on open days and in order to get your handicap you had to put in three scorecards.

I played with three of dad's friends and they all marked my card. Beforehand, Dad instructed me to shoot rounds of 89, 90 and 91 and that's exactly what I did. I received a handicap of 18 and proceeded to win three club opens at Scunthorpe, Elsham and Holme Hall.

You see, for Dad, it was crucial that I picked up some silverware at that stage of my development. Twelve probably would have been a more representative handicap for me at that age, though.

By the time I was fourteen, I was down to a four handicap. I left school a year later and then spent several months in the local steelworks and a couple of months working in a lawyer's office.

I believed all along that a career in golf was my destiny and Dad drove me down to Potters Bar for an interview for the role as Bill Shankland's assistant. There were no motorways in those days, and we drove down in a battered old Austin Seven and I got the job.

Going back to 1957 for a moment, Dad had also taken me to Lindrick for the Ryder Cup and that was another watershed moment. Thirteen is a very impressionable age and I was in awe of the world-class players I watched there.

I recall walking next to Great Britain's playing captain Dai Rees and managing to touch the grip of his club. Dai also asked me to replace a divot for him on one hole.

I was in golfing heaven and went back to Scunthorpe that night to play the best nine holes I'd ever strung together. Attending that Ryder Cup match — where Great Britain managed to secure a rare victory — was priceless for me.

It happened at a pivotal age, and I will forever be indebted to my dad for the experience. That singular moment cemented the fact that I wanted to be a golfer for the rest of my life.

Seeing all those great players at Lindrick up close and personal was an extra galvanising force and certainly inspired me to become a professional.

Fast forward sixteen years to Muirfield and our side — labelled Great Britain and Ireland for the first time — made a cracking start against a vastly experienced American team that contained giants like Nicklaus, Palmer, Trevino, Weiskopf and Casper.

I teamed up with my good mate Peter Oosterhuis on the opening day, and we halved with Chi Chi Rodriguez and Lou Graham in the morning foursomes before beating Weiskopf and Casper 3 & 1 in the afternoon fourballs.

The best performance, however, came from the two Scots: Brian Barnes and Bernard Gallacher. They led us out in both sessions and scraped a one-hole win over Trevino and Casper in the morning before demolishing Tommy Aaron and Gay Brewer 5 & 4 in the afternoon.

Our guys were buoyant as we led by 5½ points to 2½ after the opening day. Barnes and Gallacher were our version of the dynamic duo and they dovetailed perfectly.

It's so vital for a Ryder Cup captain to put two players together who have a good chemistry — and that was definitely the case for those two. The Scottish duo were good friends and there was a positive vibe all the time from the pair. They were up for the challenge and could have beaten anyone.

They helped to put is in a position of control on the opening day and it was a calamity for the team when Gallacher developed food poisoning overnight and was unable to play on the second day.

Barnes was paired with the Birmingham-born Peter Butler in the morning foursomes. They put up a good fight before going down to Nicklaus and Weiskopf by one hole.

Butler earned the distinction of recording the first-ever hole-in-one at a Ryder Cup when he aced the 16th. I smile when I think of 'Old Butty'. He had a great Brummie accent and a reputation for being a bit of a tightwad because he always used to bring his own sandwiches to the course.

I beat him in a play-off to win the 1971 Benson and Hedges International at Fulford in York after eagling the last to set up extra holes. The first prize was about £2,000 and the second £1,500.

When we stepped on the tee, 'Old Butty' asked if I wanted to split the £3,500, whatever the outcome. I gave him short shrift, "No, no, let's go for broke."

He was clearly not best pleased. "I thought someone like you might have thought differently," he replied. I don't know what he meant by that, but I guess he was referring to the fact that, as a two-time Major champion, I could afford to split the purse.

Anyhow, he and Barnesy were beaten again in the afternoon fourballs, and it was clear that the team was missing Gallacher.

Earlier on the second day, Oosterhuis and I had to take on my old nemesis Dave Hill and Arnold Palmer in the morning foursomes and we managed to beat them 2 up.

As I explained earlier in this book, there was no love lost between Hill and me. He was a good player but crazy with it. He liked to make life difficult, but it was always a good education to play him; it made me harden up and focus even more intently on the job at hand.

Hill rarely played outside America, but he turned up at Fulford one year for the B&H. Someone there asked what I thought of him, and I described him as "a miserable sod". Word got back to him, but he never cared what anyone thought of him.

Even when I won the 1970 US Open by seven shots with Hill in second position, he got all the publicity. He didn't like Hazeltine National and claimed he would have turned up with a plough to dig the place up if he had the chance.

The pair of us also clashed when the US Tour split from the Professional Golfers' Association in 1968. All the players were called to a big room for a meeting chaired by the new commissioner, Deane Beman.

Beman explained what was to happen in the future with the tour and Hill, who was sat next to me, suddenly decided to get on his feet and suggest that foreigners should not be allowed to play in the States. You can probably guess my response, "Sit down you miserable sod."

Hill, Bob Goalby, Gardner Dickinson, Howie Johnson, and to a lesser extent JC Snead, were all the same. They were okay until I won the Jacksonville Open in Florida in 1968.

That made me the first European to triumph in the States since the 1920s and from then on, their attitudes changed and there was a ton of resentment.

Back to the 1973 Ryder Cup, and Oosterhuis and I were unable to repeat our morning heroics against Hill and Palmer as we slid to a 3 & 2 defeat against Casper and Gay Brewer in the afternoon fourballs on the second day.

The two teams were locked together at 8-8 going into the two singles sessions but the Americans proved far too strong for us as they romped to a 19-13 win.

I always liked Muirfield. I thought it was the best links course we had, and the fairest. Every hole was reasonably flat in front of the green and whichever way the wind blew, you could run the ball on to the putting surface. It was a thoroughly good test of golf.

Nicklaus and Trevino also had a high regard for it. Nicklaus won The Open there in 1966 and loved the course so much that when he designed a course in Dublin, Ohio, he named it Muirfield Village in deference to the famous Scottish links.

Trevino, of course, won The Open at Muirfield in 1972 in extraordinary fashion, chipping in countless times to deny me victory.

Bernard Hunt had led our Ryder Cup team well. Jackie Burke was his opposite number and he managed to exact revenge for their 1957 defeat at Lindrick when he had also been US captain.

I always had a lot of time for Burke. He was a terrific man and full of golfing wisdom. He also loved a one-liner. My favourite was, "That putter you're using doesn't know you've just holed five 20-footers in a row."

Away from the golf, there was a lot of muttering in the media ahead of the Ryder Cup about the fact that ITV had beaten the BBC to the television rights for the first time.

There were allegations over a conflict of interest because ITV commentator John Jacobs was also on the tour committee that made the decision to deny BBC the matches.

I have to say that I never had much time for Jacobs, even though I occasionally sought him out for advice about my swing.

But the opposite was true of a guy called Maurice Bembridge. My plucky friend from Worksop was something of a journeyman professional, yet he managed to take the great Jack Nicklaus to 36 holes in the 1973 singles.

Burke described Bembridge as "a little rascal" for the way he went toe-to-toe with Nicklaus. The pair halved their first match in the morning before the 'Golden Bear' claimed a two-hole victory when they met again in the afternoon.

Bembridge wasn't a long hitter, but he was a good putter and the old adage 'the first one in wins' counts for a lot in match-play golf. He also had a fine short game and was a consistent tour player for a long time.

While he was a pal, he was also a bit of a mystery man because you never learned too much about his private life. He did get married a couple of times and made a decent living out of the game.

Bembridge smoked a pipe containing perfumed tobacco. He always had a smile on his face, had a good sense of humour and enjoyed spells living in different parts of the world.

He shot a 64 in the 1974 Masters, and if you can do that at Augusta National, you're no slouch. He had big, fat hands and never really looked comfortable on his clubs but he still picked up six European Tour wins.

It's probably fair to say Nicklaus was never a great match play exponent. Barnesy defeated him twice in a day at the 1975 Ryder Cup; I beat him and tied with him on the same day in 1969, and Bembridge ran him ever so close.

Nicklaus's record wasn't that fantastic, and he was certainly a far better performer in medal-play.

Bembridge and I spent quite a bit of time in the 1960s with 'Deadly' Hedley Muscroft and Lionel Platts, who both liked a gamble but would rarely pay their debts. You would win £100 off them, and they would turn round and say, "What would you settle for?"

Platts liked a game of cards, and we'd all have to hang around until he lost his money. He, Tommy Horton and I shared a Singer Vogue car in South Africa once during the mid-1960s.

We were in Port Elizabeth, and I was the only one insured to drive but Horton wanted to take the wheel on this particular day. He and Platts sat in the front, and I was in the back.

Horton was driving like crazy. He went too fast around one corner, ended up in a field and the car finished up on its side. We were all lucky to emerge unscathed, but the Singer Vogue was wrecked. The police arrived, and I had to take the rap and tell them I was the driver.

We made the headlines in all the local newspapers. The following week we needed to make our way to another tournament in Johannesburg. We went to rent a car, and I was asked for my name. "Tony Jacklin," I said. The reply was short and to the point. "We're not renting to you. You wrote one off last week. We'll have to let Mr Horton be the driver."

The three of us burst out laughing.

Chapter 6
1975 Matches

LAUREL VALLEY GOLF CLUB, LIGONIER, PENNSYLVANIA,
SEPTEMBER 19–21
Captains: B Hunt (GB & Ireland), A Palmer (USA)
GREAT BRITAIN & IRELAND: 11, USA: 21

Foursomes: Morning

B Barnes & B Gallacher lost to J Nicklaus & T Weiskopf 5 & 4

N Wood & M Bembridge lost to G Littler & H Irwin 4 & 3

T Jacklin & P Oosterhuis lost to A Geiberger & J Miller 3 & 1

T Horton & J O'Leary lost to L Trevino & JC Snead 2 & 1

Fourballs: Afternoon

T Jacklin & P Oosterhuis beat B Casper & R Floyd 2 & 1

E Darcy & C O'Connor Jr lost to T Weiskopf & L Graham 3 & 2

B Barnes & B Gallacher halved with J Nicklaus & B Murphy

T Horton & J O'Leary lost to L Trevino & H Irwin 2 & 1

Fourballs: Morning

T Jacklin & P Oosterhuis halved with B Casper & J Miller

T Horton & N Wood lost to J Nicklaus & JC Snead 4 & 2

B Barnes & B Gallacher lost to G Littler & L Graham 5 & 3

E Darcy & G Hunt halved with A Geiberger & R Floyd

Foursomes: Afternoon

T Jacklin & B Huggett beat L Trevino & B Murphy 3 & 2

C O'Connor Jr & J O'Leary lost to T Weiskopf & J Miller 5 & 3

P Oosterhuis & M Bembridge lost to H Irwin & B Casper 3 & 2

E Darcy & G Hunt lost to A Geiberger & L Graham 3 & 2

Singles: Morning

T Jacklin lost to B Murphy 2 & 1

P Oosterhuis beat J Miller by 2 holes

B Gallacher halved with L Trevino

T Horton halved with H Irwin

B Huggett lost to G Littler 4 & 2

E Darcy lost to B Casper 3 & 2

G Hunt lost to T Weiskopf 5 & 3

B Barnes beat J Nicklaus 4 & 2

Singles: Afternoon

T Jacklin lost to R Floyd by 1 hole

P Oosterhuis beat JC Snead 3 & 2

B Gallacher halved with A Geiberger

T Horton beat L Graham 2 & 1

J O'Leary lost to H Irwin 2 & 1

M Bembridge lost to B Murphy 2 & 1

N Wood beat L Trevino 2 & 1

B Barnes beat J Nicklaus 2 & 1

The format stayed the same for the 1975 Ryder Cup and, unsurprisingly, the outcome remained depressingly the same — we were on the receiving end of yet another shellacking

Let's take a minute to run down the American line-up. Jack Nicklaus, Lee Trevino, Johnny Miller, Ray Floyd, Tom Weiskopf, Hale Irwin, Billy Casper, Gene Littler, Lou Graham, JC Snead, Bob Murphy and Al Geiberger.

To top off that array of world-class talent, the home team had the incomparable Arnold Palmer in the driving seat as captain at the Laurel Valley Golf Club he co-founded in his native Pennsylvania.

Our Great Britain and Ireland team was skippered by Bernard Hunt for the second consecutive time and contained me, Peter Oosterhuis, Brian Barnes, Bernard Gallacher, Tommy Horton, Brian Huggett, Eamonn Darcy, Christy O'Connor Junior, Guy Hunt, John O'Leary, Maurice Bembridge and Norman Wood.

With the very best will in the world, and not wishing to appear either unkind or disrespectful to my teammates, we were on a hiding to nothing. Looking back, the only thing that shocks me is that we won as many points as we did in a 21-11 trouncing.

Laurel Valley was everything a golf and country club should be, the crowd got behind the Americans well, and we were treated with respect too. Palmer received tremendous support and his players dominated right from the off, sweeping into a 4-0 lead.

We were incapable of coming back from that and being whitewashed in the opening foursomes matches hit us like a Muhammad Ali punch to the solar plexus.

At that point in Ryder Cup history our team, especially playing away from home with Palmer as the opposition captain, would be staring down the barrel of defeat from the get-go.

You can kid yourself with a bit of bravado at times, but the reality was that our players were swatted aside by the Americans. We were just not up to it and there was little opportunity for Bernard Hunt to issue a rallying cry either.

Frustratingly, we still didn't think to organise our own team room in 1975. We might have gone to the captain's hotel suite for a gathering or two, but the players were pretty much left to their own devices, with no real chance to properly bond as a unit.

Most of our team were, and I hope I'm not out of order in saying this, journeyman professionals making up the numbers. Anyone with a semblance of golfing sense would have looked through our side and realised there was no way we could live with the Americans. It was simply not doable.

Hunt, as I've previously explained, was a genial character and he did his best with the players at his disposal. The one-sided nature of the 1975 matches was typical of the Ryder Cup matches during that decade.

I did okay, myself, picking up two-and-a-half points alongside Peter Oosterhuis and Huggett on the opening two days before, again, failing to deliver in the singles as I lost 2 & 1 to Murphy and by one hole to Floyd.

It was over as a contest before the final session and, with the destiny of the trophy already decided, there was not much of a crowd for the eight afternoon singles.

I remember Trevino complained of being exhausted, having featured in four of the five previous sessions, but Palmer insisted on 'Supermex' going out to face Wood in the penultimate match.

Trevino said he downed four beers in the locker room before taking on Wood, and with overall victory assured, he was handed two more by Palmer as the captain looked on from a hospitality pavilion by the 10th tee.

It was therefore not much of a surprise to see Trevino go down 2 & 1 to the Scottish rookie. Seven of our twelve players combined to provide just three points all week so, putting it purely and simply, we were outclassed.

Barnesy performed some heroics on the final day, beating Nicklaus 4 & 2 in the morning when, according to my Scottish mate, the two of them spent the entire round talking about their mutual love of fishing.

Nicklaus, as you can imagine, was less than pleased to lose and, with overall American victory guaranteed, the order of play was gerrymandered by the two captains to allow him a chance for revenge later in the day.

Barnes vs Nicklaus was the match that kept alive the interest of the fans on the final afternoon and, blow me down, the big, pipe-smoking Scot only went on to defy the odds yet again.

He made it two victories in a day against the greatest player in the world, winning 2 & 1, and quite rightly received all the plaudits at the end of the matches.

Nicklaus told him at the start, "There's no way you can beat me a second time," and he looked as if he was going to back up his pledge when he began with birdies at the opening two holes of the afternoon round.

But Barnesy clawed his way back to finish on top and was just a few feet away in the clubhouse later when Nicklaus hurled his golf shoes at his own locker in disgust.

"Anything wrong, Jack?" Barnesy enquired. Nicklaus' to-the-point reply is probably best left to the imagination before he went on to say, "Come on, Brian, let's go and have a beer."

Palmer tried to tease Nicklaus at the closing ceremony, claiming that his great friend and rival didn't mind losing. Nicklaus, grinning from ear to ear, rose instantly from his chair and bellowed, "Oh yes, I do!".

Personally speaking, the most memorable thing about the week was losing the sole of my shoe midway through the singles match against Floyd. I had a contract with FootJoy at the time, but all our players were allocated these two-tone brown and white shoes that, as far as I was concerned, were third-rate.

The soles were welded to the uppers and as I finished my swing on the 12th or 13th hole, I can't remember which, and dragged my toe around, the top separated from the bottom.

If there was ever a moment when my self-esteem was affected at a Ryder Cup, it would be that one. It was a total embarrassment. I couldn't continue with the shoes and had to sprint off to the clubhouse to get a replacement pair.

Those two-tone shoes were typical of the third-rate gear that used to be distributed to the Britain and Ireland team back then. It was basically a case of accepting anything a company would hand out to us.

The clothing contracts were agreed by officialdom. There was a Ryder Cup committee back then, not like now when it's all decided by the powerful Tournament Committee of players.

Once, I recall, we had to go around in blazers with braiding around the edges — we looked like members of Jack Hylton's Dance Band rather than a team of elite golfers.

That sort of thing was so demoralising. I was reasonably well off in those days; I had the best of everything — whether it was clothes or cars — and I took pride in my attire.

Playing in the Ryder Cup did nothing for my self-confidence. I didn't need the painful lessons I was receiving back then — I knew inside how it should have been done — but it was why I insisted on only the very best clothing for my players when I eventually became captain.

It was a joke in the Seventies. You inevitably thought, "Now what?" every time you turned up for the matches. We were dealing with incompetence and, for us players, it felt like we went into battle with one arm tied behind our backs.

I don't even know if the captains were consulted about the clothing in those days. I'm sure it was presented as a fait accompli by the time they got involved.

I imagine Bernard Hunt would simply be told, "The guys are wearing this on Friday, that on Saturday and this on Sunday."

The guy in charge of FootJoy in America at that time was Dick Tarlow and whenever I was in Boston, I'd go down to his factory.

All the players were on good terms with Dick, but I was a double Major winner, and he took good care of me.

FootJoy produced the best golf shoes money could buy, in my opinion. Their products were made from alligator skin and were worth around $2,000 a pair.

I don't think Dick ever paid me but that was the brand I always wore, and the firm used to kindly allow me fifty per cent off.

There is another company in America, Johnston and Murphy, who make good-quality shoes, but it was FootJoy who had the reputation among the players back then.

As I explained earlier, it was disappointing to lose twice on the last day and, in truth, my career singles record in the Ryder Cup wasn't what I wanted it to be.

As a team, we really didn't have a prayer that week, especially as Palmer's presence and charisma dominated the show. It was around this time that the Americans were struggling to maintain interest in the competition, hence some behind-the-scenes rumblings about what could be done to give the event a kick up the backside.

My good friend Tommy Horton was renowned for slipping an occasional malapropism into a conversation and he would have said, "It's a foregone confusion for our team Tony."

Horton had a pretty good record in The Open, finishing in the top 10 four times. He and O'Connor were among four Hunt selections in 1975.

Oosty and I were both playing predominantly in the States at that stage, and the pair of us also needed a wild card to get into the side.

I think Horton was around 17 when we first met. The pair of us travelled to South Africa together in the 1960s, and he also lived in Jersey at the same time as my late wife Vivien and I did.

Then, in the 1990s, Horton and his wife Helen would come and stay with Astrid and me whenever he travelled over to the States.

Horton and Barnesy were what were known as 'Butten Boys' during the 1960s.

Ernest Butten, a prominent businessman, put together a group of around eight British professionals. He funded a residential golf school in Kent and gave Max Faulkner, the flamboyant 1951 Open champion, the job as a teaching pro.

Butten paid all his guys around £25 a week — which is probably worth around £500 a week today — and at the end of every round the players would gather together and explain which side of the fairway they missed on, the side of the green they found, how many times they made the putting surface in regulation, how many putts they missed to the left, how many they missed to the right.

He asked me to join his group, but I didn't want to be part of something I felt was a little bit too regimented. I wanted to go my own way and, as it turned out, I was more successful than any of his protégés.

I have to say it was quite a tempting offer. None of us had any money at that time and it was something I had to think seriously about. In the end, though, I was bloody glad I said "no".

It was a bit like the college system they have here in the States. If you sign up, you have to do whatever the coach tells you, no discussions or arguments. That was the issue that swayed me because there was no way I wanted to be part of a regime.

Sir Nick Faldo was once given a scholarship to the University of Houston and lasted ten weeks. That sort of approach didn't suit him, and I don't think it would have done much for me either.

The whole system was about toeing the line. I guess Butten had seen what was going on in America and wanted to set up something similar in Britain. As far as I could tell, he wanted everything written down so that it was clear which weaknesses the players needed to work on.

I didn't need an outsider to organise that sort of thing for me because I did it anyway, plus I was a non-conformist. I was very independent. I left home at 17 and got married to Vivien at 21.

But picking up £25 a week would have been quite profitable for a young, aspiring pro. My dad never earned that much in his entire life. He was on £10 a week at the local steelworks in Scunthorpe.

After I won The Open in 1969, I would send my parents £25 each week and, to further prove that it was a decent sum to be stuffing in your pocket back then, the top football stars of the era would have been on that sort of money.

As well as Tommy Horton, it was also John O'Leary's first Ryder Cup appearance in 1975. The Irishman was something of a wild boy back then — perhaps that's why he ended up on the Tournament Committee!

Somehow, bad boys always seemed to prosper under chief executive Ken Schofield. O'Leary was a bit of a rebel too. He loved his wine, smoking pot, and certainly, he got up to mischief from time to time.

I remember O'Leary being banned from representative teams in December 1974 for a misdemeanour he committed in Jamaica. He also had a big mop of curly hair, so he tended to stand out in a crowd.

I can't remember why he was suspended but I reckon all the players in our 1975 Ryder Cup side must have known the reason. Knowing him as I do, and O'Leary was a pal of mine, he probably walked through a bar naked.

The South African professional Simon Hobday, who was always something of an eccentric, did that once during a tournament at Cranssur-Sierre in Switzerland. The bar staff ordered him to put on his pants and he promptly stuck them on his head.

Going back to O'Leary, I recall Peter Townsend telling me a story once. The pair of them had been out drinking, and O'Leary suddenly got up in the middle of the night, didn't have a clue what he was doing, and decided to relieve himself in the corner of the hotel room they were sharing.

O'Leary wound up as the head of the Tournament Committee, making many important decisions on behalf of the European Tour.

The Dubliner, who sadly died in 2020, and I spent a lot of time together. We shared some good memories, especially in South Africa, where his wife Ingrid — who was also a bit wild — came from.

We were at the Holiday Inn's tournament in Swaziland in the 1970s along with Dr Christiaan Barnard, the man who performed the world's first heart transplant. The doctor used to be a keen golfer and the three of us played together in the pro-am event.

We all ate out every evening and enjoyed each other's company. Swaziland was a great place to visit and the guy who owned the hotel that we stayed in that week — Laurence Parry — now lives near me in Bradenton in Florida.

Parry was very good to us out there. He gave us the best rooms; the food was great and there was a real party atmosphere in the evenings. He went on to own the Holiday Inn in Sarasota and made millions when he sold the land in 2002.

Coincidentally, 2002 was also the year I met Kevin Daves, the guy who built the Concession Golf Club that I co-designed with Jack Nicklaus in the Lakewood Ranch section of Manatee County, east of Bradenton.

The project was my brainchild. After I stopped playing on the Seniors Tour, I needed something to do — a new purpose, a fresh mission. I literally sat up in bed in the middle of the night, one night, and said, "I've got it. I'll build a championship golf course, call it The Concession and get my teeth stuck into it!"

I knew Nicklaus was being courted to build a golf component at the Ritz Carlton Hotel complex in nearby Sarasota, so I went along to the opening armed with a photo of him and me walking off the green at Royal Birkdale in 1969.

I told Daves, "Perhaps if you build more than one golf course here, you could consider building a second one and call it The Concession to mark one of golf's most iconic moments."

He loved the idea but what I didn't know was that he was busy suing his Ritz Carlton partners, the Buford Brothers, at the time, and until the litigation was settled, he didn't want to start any other project.

In the end, because of the lawsuit, it fell upon the Buford Brothers to build the golf component at the Ritz Carlton, and they gave the design contract to the famous architect Tom Fazio.

The Ritz Carlton facility is now about a mile from The Concession as the crow flies. It's like a Millionaire's Row of Golf with both being top-notch, high-end developments.

When the lawsuit was settled, Daves and I went to see Nicklaus to outline our proposal. I was quite happy for Nicklaus to design the course, but he said, "No, let's do it together."

It ended up as a Jack Nicklaus-designed layout developed in association with Tony Jacklin. There was plenty of fanfare and publicity generated when the two of us played an exhibition to open the course in 2006.

I was supposed to get a five per cent stake in The Concession but, ultimately, I ended up earning a couple of hundred thousand dollars from being an ambassador for a few years.

My contract was tied in with the number of members the facility attracted but they didn't build a clubhouse for five years and, without that, you're never going to get many members.

The Concession was named by *Golf Digest* as the best new private course in America in 2006. It's a fabulous thing to be associated with and to look back on, because it turned into a very successful project and a seriously good course.

Chapter 7
1977 Matches

ROYAL LYTHAM & ST ANNES, SEPTEMBER 15–17
Captains: B Huggett (GB & Ireland), D Finsterwald (USA)
GREAT BRITAIN & IRELAND: 7½, USA: 12½

Foursomes:

B Gallacher & B Barnes lost to L Wadkins & H Irwin 3 & 1

N Coles & P Dawson lost to D Stockton & J McGee by 1 hole

N Faldo & P Oosterhuis beat R Floyd & L Graham 2 & 1

T Jacklin & E Darcy halved with E Sneed & D January

T Horton & M James lost to J Nicklaus & T Watson 5 & 4

Fourballs:

B Barnes & T Horton lost to T Watson & H Green 5 & 4

N Coles & P Dawson lost to L Wadkins & E Sneed 5 & 3

N Faldo & P Oosterhuis beat J Nicklaus & R Floyd 3 & 1

T Jacklin & E Darcy lost to D Hill & D Stockton 5 & 3

M James & K Brown lost to H Irwin & L Graham by 1 hole

Singles:

H Clark lost to L Wadkins 4 & 3

N Coles lost to L Graham 5 & 3

P Dawson beat D January 5 & 4

B Barnes beat H Irwin by 1 hole

T Horton lost to D Hill 5 & 4

B Gallacher beat J Nicklaus by 1 hole

E Darcy lost to H Green by 1 hole

M James lost to R Floyd 2 & 1

N Faldo beat T Watson by 1 hole

P Oosterhuis beat J McGee by 2 holes

I was an extremely unhappy individual during the 1977 edition, and it was, without a question of doubt, the worst Ryder Cup I ever experienced.

Brian Huggett took charge of the Great Britain and Ireland team, and he was a terrible captain. He seemed to think that he had to totally change his character that week, and it didn't work at all.

He became aloof and standoffish, decided not to mix with the players and, yet again, we got brushed aside by a classy American team that was superior in every department at Royal Lytham.

It was not a week I look back at with any fondness at all. Huggett and I had a blazing row on the course in full view of the crowd and the whole thing was a truly unedifying spectacle.

The officials, who at this stage were desperate to finally make some sort of a competitive contest out of the Ryder Cup, made sweeping changes to the format and opted to cut the schedule to five foursomes matches, five fourballs and 10 singles — which meant two players on each side had to be left out of the final session, a ludicrous state of affairs in my opinion.

I don't know who was making the rules, the US PGA, the British PGA or a combination of the two, but despite a spectacular debut by future world number one Faldo, it was another case of the Americans kicking our butts.

We tried our best to put on a show, but we were pretty much beaten before we had started. It felt like it was a lost cause from the beginning, and it was a stupid idea not to have everyone featuring in the singles. Huggett and I were friends leading up to the 1977 Ryder Cup and we had been Ryder Cup partners several times previously.

I had high regard for the way he performed in the tied matches at Birkdale eight years earlier. He was always a tenacious little so-and-so on the golf course, a real battler, but unfortunately, our relationship was to take a serious nosedive.

I don't know what got into him that week. It went wrong right from the start when Bernard Gallacher and I invited him to join our wives and us for dinner one night and, instead of stopping, he simply waved at us dismissively and carried on walking with his wife to another table.

He seemed to become a different individual altogether and our relationship got so bad that we fell out and he eventually dropped me from the singles, without so much as an explanation.

No one on our team came close to my playing pedigree. No one else had won a Major championship by then — I'd picked up two — but Huggett never even told me he was going to leave me out for the final session.

I don't think I was the only one unhappy with the situation. None of us received any information from him at all that week. He seemed to spend all his time with wife Winnie.

Huggett was a big football fan, he supported Crystal Palace, I think, and it looked like he was trying to treat us in the same manner that football managers dealt with their players during that era.

The first time I realised I wasn't playing in the singles was when the draw was made public. Oosty said: "This is ridiculous, laughable. Tony won The Open here in 1969 and we've decided not to play him."

I always loved Lytham. It was where I launched my professional career in earnest by making the cut at the 1963 Open and it was where I won the Pringle of Scotland tournament by four strokes in 1967.

It was one of my favourite courses in the world and it was a proud moment when, in 2019, they made me an honorary member, especially as they don't have many of those at Lytham.

Looking back at 1977, though, I do still get irritated when I think of the way Huggett did things. Eamonn Darcy and I were thrown together that week without either of us knowing we were going to be partners.

Huggett never had the courtesy to tell us. If he had bothered to come up to me and explain his thinking, I'd have said, "Okay, I respect your view, but I'd rather play with someone else if you don't mind."

Darcy was a nice guy and had an agricultural sort of swing. We got on perfectly well but there was no spark or chemistry between us.

Perhaps Darcy was waiting for me to light up the course, but we didn't gel and were smashed 5 & 3 by the two Daves — Hill and Stockton — in the fourballs. We gave 100 per cent and it wasn't good enough.

The pair of us then did what all good teammates should do — cheer on and support our colleagues.

The captain, though, came up and started shouting at us, in full view of the galleries, "Why aren't you two practising?"

He had no business talking to us like that and I wasn't going to stand there quietly so I gave it to him with both barrels.

I told him, "This isn't Crystal Palace Football Club you're running; this is a team of golfers." I went on to tell him exactly what I thought of him, and we went at it hammer and tongs. I'm glad I did it; I didn't regret it for a second.

Darcy and I were doing the right thing and we were getting verbally abused for it by our own captain — staggering.

That was a really low point for me in terms of my Ryder Cup career. Having to deal with Huggett was a nightmare. He was on his high horse all week and it was glaringly obvious to all our players.

But I had given him a piece of my mind in full view of the crowd. He was mad at me; I was mad at him, so we were even.

I did, however, learn a lot in terms of what not to do as captain. As someone who had competed at the very highest level, it was clear to me that to get the best out of a player, you needed to be his best friend.

By the time I took the reins I was no longer a player, I was the captain, a psychologist, and the very last thing I wanted to do was fall out with anyone in my camp. You want to give everyone the best opportunity to play their best.

In later years, after my successes as captain, Huggett's friends would joke about it. They'd come up to me and say, "Brian doesn't know if you're still talking to him after what happened at Lytham, Tone."

It's all water under the bridge, now. I don't bear any grudges — there are more important things to worry about.

My view of Huggett's opposite number on the American team was completely different. I had a soft spot for Dow Finsterwald because he was the first guy I saw in action after running through the gates with my dad at the 1957 Ryder Cup at Lindrick.

I got to know Finsterwald well when I started living in America because he used to come to my neighbour's tournament down here in Florida. He lived near Arnold Palmer at Bay Hill, and I always found him to be a very pleasant companion.

The Ryder Cup was on a severe downward spiral by 1977. My good friend, 1973 Open champion Tom Weiskopf, was so uninspired by the thought of travelling to Lytham for the matches that he opted out and decided instead to go game hunting in Alaska.

Weiskopf's decision to spurn the opportunity to represent the Americans signalled the beginning of the end for the competition, in that guise anyway. It was withering on the vine at that point, no doubt about it.

It's probably fair to say my interest in the Ryder Cup was waning too. I'm not boasting but I had far away the best CV on our team, and I was getting tired of being kicked in the butt by the Americans every couple of years.

And if I had known how Huggett and I would get on, I would have joined Weiskopf in Alaska! Our captain that year never promoted a feeling of team unity. It was a farcical situation, and I couldn't wait to get out of there when the matches were all over.

It was hard to get excited at that stage, knowing we would lose however well I played.

We couldn't win, and you develop a demoralised feeling — that was the overriding sensation. I had shown many times in my career that I was a winner and I always wanted to win.

But when, as a team, you are pitted against opposition with vastly better skills, there is little enjoyment to be had.

Despite their overwhelming superiority, the Americans were bored too, and I'm sure many of their players would have thought, *"What a waste of time that was"* come the end of the week.

It was Jack Nicklaus who saved the day. The British PGA had been the trustees of the famous Ryder Cup trophy since it was donated by Samuel Ryder to mark the biennial contests.

One of the PGA's most famous members, Abe Mitchell, is the figure depicted at the top of the 17-inch trophy. He takes pride of place because of his friendship with Samuel Ryder, who appointed him in 1925 — two years before the inaugural matches — as his personal golf instructor.

After our defeat in 1977, the influential Nicklaus never consulted anyone on our side of the pond, but he decided to write to Lord Derby, the head of the British PGA, to suggest including the likes of Seve Ballesteros and making us Team Europe rather than Great Britain and Ireland.

Spanish pair Seve and Antonio Garrido joined our team two years later at The Greenbrier in West Virginia.

Nicklaus was on pretty good terms with Lord Derby. I recall being in their company a few times and he would refer to him by his name, John. They were friends, and it was right to bring Europe in at that point.

Seve had burst on the scene a couple of years before, and that would have influenced Nicklaus. It was quite obvious that our team would be stronger with the Europeans on board.

Playing under Huggett, who treated his players as if they were his schoolchildren in 1977, was in stark contrast to how situations were handled by other captains such as Eric Brown.

Even with the Rolls-Royce incident in 1971, he came over, told me what he had to tell me, and I put my hands up and said, "Sorry, I won't do it again."

I walked away from that conversation still on good terms with Brown. There was no lingering animosity. Brown did what he had to do, and I probably would have done precisely the same in his shoes.

While Huggett was a massive negative at Lytham, there was no question who the biggest positive influence to emerge that week was: young Mr Faldo.

I already knew he was a talented player and the following year he won our PGA Championship — the European Tour's flagship event —

at Birkdale. Nick was an absolutely fantastic putter and that's an element of his game I can't emphasise enough.

He had a bit of a loop at the top of his backswing and, after winning several tournaments, including two more PGA Championships at Sandwich and Ganton in 1980 and 1981, he was ultra-ambitious.

Three PGA titles were almost like nothing to Nick; he wanted to bag the 'Big Four' trophies. He worked really hard to remodel his swing with David Leadbetter and wound up winning six Majors — a fantastic achievement.

In his own mind, he believed he'd never be able to scale the heights unless he addressed what he thought was a swing fault.

When Nick won The Open for the first time at Muirfield in 1987 and gave all the credit to Leadbetter, that was the moment he opened the floodgates for a load of new golf coaches to emerge on the scene — he started it all off, no doubt about it. It was now the done thing.

I always wondered what made a great putter and Nick was certainly in that bracket. Perhaps it was because I'd become something of a basket case on the greens by 1982 — that's why I stopped playing competitive golf — but I was always drawn to great putters.

Nick was a magnificent putter — you have to be to win six Majors, and I think that maybe he took that element of his game for granted and felt he needed to focus on improving his swing.

He was really meticulous about the way he swung the club. I wasn't like that at all; I was a feel player. But the work ethic he showed in achieving a remodelled action told you a lot about how his mind worked.

We've seen all sorts of unorthodox swings down the years, those of Eamonn Darcy and Jim Furyk come to mind, and young American Matt Wolff now certainly does it in a very unconventional fashion.

Hogan's was the best, and I was thankful for the chance to have played with him. Nick, though, always had amazing rhythm — you never saw him rush his swing.

I remember playing with Faldo at a tournament just outside London in 1976, at Moor Park. Seve was in our group too, and I could see that day Nick would go on to be a damned fine player.

He always had great mental strength and didn't mind being a loner on tour. He had an obsession to become the best and was determined to reach the targets he set himself.

Nick and I have always got on well. We are still in regular touch now. He was honoured at Jack Nicklaus' Memorial Tournament in Dublin, Ohio a few years ago and asked me to speak for him, which I was happy to do.

Nick talked about his chest alignment and what all sorts of different parts of his body were doing as he swung the club — things I never dreamed of considering. When he used to explain to me what he was trying to do I used to think, *"What the hell is he on about?"*

He even mentioned belt buckles with reference to his swing. Belt buckles? I can assure you they never entered my thought processes. His whole approach to the game was so much more complex than mine.

I wanted simplicity. He wanted technical. It's fascinating how different strategies and mindsets can succeed in our sport.

I always go back to Nick's putting prowess, though. Who could ever forget that look of shock on his face when he ran one in from right across the green at the second play-off hole to pip Scott Hoch at the 1989 Masters?

I played with him in the 2003 UBS Cup at Sea Island, Georgia and by then his putting had gone. He would blast them and make things worse by trying too hard. He struggled as he got older, but that didn't matter because his putting was top-notch when it needed to be — in his prime.

When Nick decided to change his swing, I thought, *"Why the hell would he want to do that?"* But different things drive different people and that ended up being the making of him.

Leadbetter is another friend of mine, but you could stand on the driving range with him as coach and hear him tell his player 20 different things. He also worked with Nick Price, who won The Open in 1994, and I asked the Zimbabwean golfer once, "How do you cope with all the instructions he gives you?"

Price replied, "I just pick out the one element I want and ignore the other stuff."

Faldo fixed himself up with the right guy. Theirs was a marriage made in golfing heaven and it worked a treat.

Chapter 8
1979 Matches

THE GREENBRIER, WHITE SULPHUR SPRINGS, WEST
VIRGINIA, SEPT 14–16
Captains: J Jacobs (Europe), B Casper (USA)

EUROPE: 11, USA: 17

Fourballs: Morning
S Ballesteros & A Garrido lost to L Wadkins & L Nelson 2 & 1
K Brown & M James lost to L Trevino & F Zoeller 3 & 2
P Oosterhuis & N Faldo lost to A Bean & L Elder 2 & 1
B Gallacher & B Barnes beat H Irwin & J Mahaffey 2 & 1

Foursomes: Afternoon
K Brown & D Smyth lost to H Irwin & T Kite 7 & 6
S Ballesteros & A Garrido beat F Zoeller & H Green 3 & 2
T Jacklin & S Lyle halved with L Trevino & G Morgan
B Gallacher & B Barnes lost to L Wadkins & L Nelson 4 & 3

Foursomes: Morning
T Jacklin & S Lyle beat L Elder & J Mahaffey 5 & 4
N Faldo & P Oosterhuis beat A Bean & T Kite 6 & 5
B Gallacher & B Barnes beat F Zoeller & M Hayes 2 & 1
S Ballesteros & A Garrido lost to L Wadkins & L Nelson 3 & 2

Fourballs: Afternoon
S Ballesteros & A Garrido lost to L Wadkins & L Nelson 5 & 4

T Jacklin & S Lyle lost to H Irwin & T Kite by 1 hole
B Gallacher & B Barnes beat L Trevino & F Zoeller 3 & 2
N Faldo & P Oosterhuis beat L Elder & M Hayes by 1 hole

Singles: Morning
B Gallacher beat L Wadkins 3 & 2
S Ballesteros lost to L Nelson 3 & 2
T Jacklin lost to T Kite by 1 hole
A Garrido lost to M Hayes by 1 hole
M King lost to A Bean 4 & 3
B Barnes lost to J Mahaffey by 1 hole

Singles: Afternoon
N Faldo beat L Elder 3 & 2
D Smyt lost to H Irwin 5 & 3
P Oosterhuis lost to H Green by 2 holes
K Brown beat F Zoeller by 1 hole
S Lyle lost to L Trevino 2 & 1
M James halved with G Morgan (match not played)

If partnering the supremely gifted Sandy Lyle was the highlight of my 1979 Ryder Cup adventure, then having to endure the yobbish behaviour of Mark James and Ken Brown was undoubtedly the downside of the week.

Teaming up with Sandy was a real thrill. There aren't many players who were blessed with as much natural talent as he had and we did reasonably well by picking up one-and-a-half points from our three matches together, including handing out a 5 & 4 drubbing to Lee Elder and John Mahaffey.

Everything that week, though, was completely overshadowed by the schoolboy antics of James and Brown.

The pair didn't stand to attention for the national anthems, they put magazines in front of their faces when photographers were trying to take pictures and there was another time when our team had to autograph a

Ryder Cup menu for a priest and one signature said, 'Mark James, Son of a Bitch'.

The two guys deserved the whopping fines that were dished out — the biggest in the history of the game at that point — £1,500 to James and £1,000 to Brown.

Everyone was disappointed with it, the players on both teams, not just on ours, and it did nothing to help the overall cause with the Ryder Cup already dying a death because of the persistent beatings the Americans were giving us.

Seve Ballesteros and his fellow Spaniard Antonio Garrido joined our side for this edition — the first under a Team Europe flag and captained by John Jacobs — but I'm afraid it made no difference to the outcome.

Seve, who had won The Open at Royal Lytham earlier in the year, was a great match-play competitor throughout his career. For some reason, though, he failed to fire and only managed to pick up one point on his Ryder Cup debut.

The Americans were without Jack Nicklaus for the first time in a long while, and Tom Watson had to drop out on the eve of the matches because his wife was due to give birth.

Some of their players would have been forgiven for thinking, *"If their guys don't give a monkey's about the competition, why should we?"*

If it had been down to me, James and Brown would never have played in the Ryder Cup again. But they were somehow rewarded for their actions by being drafted on to the all-powerful Tournament Committee of European Tour players soon after, with James becoming chairman.

James also, of course, went on to receive the ultimate honour by being appointed captain for the 1999 matches at Brookline, Massachusetts.

I never wanted to see the pair of them again after what they did in 1979 but, of course, the two of them eventually played under me when I was captain and, I have to say, they didn't give me a moment's trouble.

Perhaps you could put their earlier misdemeanours down to a lack of maturity. To this day, I find it difficult to forgive what they did at The

Greenbrier, and it led to a ding-dong between James and me when the Ryder Cup was held at the K Club in Ireland in 2006.

I went into the captain's room, where there were four or five guys present, shook a couple of hands before offering the same to James. But, upset by my honest account of his 1979 behaviour in a recent book, he said, "I'm not shaking your hand."

I went within six inches of his face and said, "Do you actually think it didn't happen, then?" He reacted by turning around and walking straight out of the room.

James and I have rarely seen eye to eye. I'm sure now that they are older and wiser, the pair of them are sorry it happened.

Brown has definitely mellowed down the years. He and I get on okay and he was in touch in 2020 to let me know that he was trying to organise a reunion of our triumphant 1985 and 1987 Ryder Cup teams.

It's ever so sad that Seve and Gordon Brand junior are no longer around. I told Ken I wouldn't be there either because I had no intention of flying during the coronavirus pandemic. I'm in the high-risk category so I had no choice but to maintain a low profile.

Matters with James weren't helped in 1981 when, faced with a choice of picking him or me for the Ryder Cup, Jacobs decided to leave me out.

But you must find a way of moving on. You can't bear grudges forever. In golf, you'll always bump into someone at a function; you might even have to sit next to someone you'd rather not have to.

Mark and I were certainly civil enough the last time we bumped into each other, which I think occurred during the 2016 Ryder Cup at Hazeltine National.

I also didn't agree with some of the things he did as the captain at Brookline in 1999, leaving out the two rookies — Andrew Coltart and Jean Van de Velde — until the final day was a bit odd.

Peter Oosterhuis and I were on commentary duty for Sky Sports, and we were both very surprised at the order he put the players out, too.

Before a shot was struck in anger on the Sunday, Oosty and I were saying, "If Darren Clarke and Lee Westwood don't win the opening two matches, we are going to be in trouble." They both lost and suddenly all the momentum was with the Americans.

Having compiled a 10-6 lead going into the singles, I felt Europe should have tried to power it out with their strongest players at the top of the order — not just Westwood and Clarke but Jose Maria Olazabal and Colin Montgomerie as well, but the last two went out at numbers nine and 10.

As I mentioned earlier in this book, I had a lot of sympathy for the captain in 1979. Jacobs was a gentle sort, not the type to grab an offender by the collar and have a proper falling out.

But my sympathy for Jacobs completely evaporated two years later when he left me out for the 1981 Ryder Cup. Seve was also controversially omitted, having been involved in a long-running dispute with the European Tour over appearance money.

I don't know if Seve was given an explanation, but I didn't get so much as a phone call to inform me that my services would not be required.

It's true to say that, even though I went on to win our PGA Championship at Hillside, Southport in 1982, I was winding down my career in the early Eighties. Nevertheless, I still believed my playing record meant I merited a spot in the team.

Seve was incensed at being left out and of course it was a political decision. The powers-that-be at the European Tour didn't know how to handle him. All they needed to do, in my opinion, was to sit him down and talk about the way forward.

There was a move to oust chief executive Ken Schofield in the Nineties and a ballot was held.

I was living in America at that time and Seve, Langer, Faldo and Olazabal wanted me to come home and be the Tour's frontman, a sort of door-opener.

I didn't have the business acumen to run the organisation, but I wouldn't have minded being the talisman if that could help.

There was a lot of protectionism going on. Ken had surrounded himself with grateful people. The Tour had become a bit of a closed shop and some of us never got to know what was going on behind the scenes.

One thing I found strange is that when the vote came in, it was the guys who had tried to oust Ken who were suddenly being criticised by the media. They came down on us like a ton of bricks.

Looking back, the episode saddens me now, especially the way the whole thing was done. I was broke around that time, having been one of the 'Lloyd's Names' who had lost everything and more in the financial crash. In the end, I had to borrow a fortune to pay off my debts.

Having long since given up the golfing ghost, I had to get back out there again to play on the US Seniors Tour. But, in retrospect, it was almost a good thing. It became a new challenge; I practised hard, I got fit. I won a couple of times and, ultimately, I was grateful for the opportunity to come and live here in Florida.

It was something I should have done in my prime but my manager, Mark McCormack, said I had an obligation to play in Europe and that meant I ended up travelling back and forth between both circuits and getting caught between two stools.

The Greenbrier was a wonderful venue for the 1979 Ryder Cup and the players were treated really well. Astrid and I lived there in later years. They call it 'America's Resort', there are a host of activities available including three or four golf courses.

The greens, though, were lightning-quick for our matches. They got them as fast as they could because our players were not used to those sorts of speeds at that time. We didn't have truly international stars like we have now.

Seve and Antonio were brought in but the whole operation was much the same as it had been for years — we were begging, stealing and borrowing our clothes, equipment and caddies. Jacobs did exactly what Bernard Hunt did before him and what Eric Brown did before Bernard.

Most of our players had never seen such slick greens; the Americans would've polished them if they could. It was a sizeable advantage to their team playing on putting surfaces that were like Augusta National without the undulations.

I don't recall any antagonism towards Seve, but I do remember something Larry Nelson said about him, which was along the lines of, "Everybody played their best against Seve because everybody wanted to beat him so bad."

Seve was a bit like Nick Faldo, extremely single-minded and desperate to win. He didn't care what people thought about him either. He was such a great competitor and always pushed himself.

Lanny Wadkins did well for the home team that week, picking up four points, but Larry Nelson was the outstanding performer with five out of five. I always rated Larry as one of the game's most underrated golfers.

He won three Major championships despite only taking up the game in his early twenties. He was also a prolific winner when he joined the seniors and I found him a charming companion.

Nelson's name is not one that generally jumps out when people talk about the greats, but I can't think of anyone who was more underrated than him. He was a quality player. He should have been a Ryder Cup captain, too and was strangely overlooked.

Winning the US PGA Championship is normally a criterion for the captain's role. He won that tournament twice and was still snubbed. He was always very quiet and unassuming and went quietly about his business but, boy, he could certainly play.

There were a load of rookies in the American team in 1979 — eight of them — but it's fair to say the pressure on newcomers then wasn't anything like what it is for the modern-day player.

The interest in the Ryder Cup just wasn't there, it wasn't as popular, the galleries were nothing like those we have become used to now and, to all intents and purposes, the rookies could look upon the week as just another regular tour event.

Des Smyth and Peter Oosterhuis were our two wild-card choices and that was something I never agreed with. I always wanted at least three of my own picks, preferably four, because you need to know as a captain that you've got the strongest twelve players at your disposal.

I'd rather put a champion out twice than play someone who played a lot of tournaments and accumulated counting points to get in the team. The ninth, tenth, eleventh and twelfth members of your team are always going to be the weak links in your line-up.

After my four matches as captain, my successor Bernard Gallacher went back to two wild-card selections. His mentality was that if you qualify, you deserve to be in the team.

I never went along with that thinking. In my case, it was all about doing everything in my power to win, and I always wanted the best men out there to do that job for me.

Lyle won two Majors, of course, and he was as talented as they come. He had been a good friend for a while, and I can't think of anyone who had as much ability as he had.

Peter Alliss once described him as having "nonchalant power" and that just about summed it up. He had a shortish backswing, but he generated awesome strength through his legs.

I recall a discussion we had on a par-five hole at The Greenbrier. It was a foursomes match and I hit a good drive off the tee. Sandy waited till I got to the ball before turning around and saying, "What club do you think I should take for this shot?"

I replied: "If it was me, I'd go with a two-iron and get as much elevation on it as I can."

Sandy then said, "So, that's a four-iron for me then." He was two clubs stronger than me, his hands were so fast through the ball, and he was right — the four-iron was perfect for him.

I honestly don't know why he bothered to use the longest club in the bag. He had a Ping one-iron that went as far as my driver — 260, 270 yards — and it was a favourite club for him.

Sandy wasn't the world's best putter, though. Lee Trevino once said, "God never gave one man everything," and he was right. No golfer has attained perfection in my time in the game, but Ben Hogan and Tiger Woods have come the closest.

I've watched Tiger so much on television and never had the opportunity to play with him. I did get the chance to play with Hogan when he was past his best, which was a helluva experience.

I think Ben was in his sixties when he admitted that nobody ever conquers our game; as an individual, you just attempt to get as close as you can to your best. The run that Tiger had around the year 2000 was amazing and the mental strength he showed was immense.

Michael Campbell won the US Open in 2005 and played a lot of golf with Tiger when he was at his very best. I've had quite a few conversations with the New Zealander in recent years, and he has let me in on a few secrets.

Campbell described Tiger as being "on a different planet" mentally. Apparently, he used to count how many steps he took in a minute and time how long it took for a putt to reach the hole, stuff like that, in order to keep his concentration and focus at 100 per cent.

It was also noticeable to me watching on television how many times Tiger blinked on the first tee: he was like a giraffe, slow blinking like he was getting into some sort of trance.

Powerful mental exercises like that were a key part of Tiger's domination. It was extraordinary to watch and took me back to when I was a young man coming into the game, knowing that the key to becoming a great player is having a strong mind.

When I was a kid, I used to look through books to see if I could find an edge somewhere. There were no sports psychologists back then — mine was a glass of Johnnie Walker scotch.

A guy called Timothy Gallwey wrote about the inner game of tennis in 1974 and also did the same for golf in later years. He talked about the invisible man sitting on a sportsman's shoulder, always whispering the negatives.

They are the type of weaknesses that must be unexposed because everyone has them. The elite players now seem to have mastered that way of thinking and I guess the sports psychologists have been a big help in that regard.

In golf, when you get a chance to win Majors, that's when you get found out. It is a game of truth and when you have to deal with intense pressure on the final day, with everything on the line, that's when it all comes home to roost.

That's when you discover if you have really put the time in and whether you truly deserve to win. As an individual, these are the questions you are being asked, and with all the nervous tension that's also flying around, it can lead to implosion.

I believe there's no game like golf, apart from boxing, perhaps. Those moments are when you really have nowhere to hide. It wasn't the case in my playing days, but the same factors apply in the Ryder Cup now as they do in the Majors.

The Ryder Cup provides the ultimate test of whether a player is able to handle pressure; there's no arena quite like it. The Majors represent the greatest examination as an individual but when it comes to team golf and you're playing just as much for others as you are for yourself, you better make sure you have your 'A' game... or else.

Lyle certainly passed the test with that unforgettable seven-iron from the fairway bunker at the 72nd hole that set him up for his Masters victory at Augusta in 1988.

That's an extremely difficult stroke to pull off with everything on the line and only someone with his ability is capable of doing what he did. The most important thing was to get the ball up fast and clear the lip of the bunker.

To get the elevation was critical, and it has to go down as one of the greatest shots of all time. Seve achieved something similar, with a three-wood from the sand at the last hole helping him to achieve a remarkable half with Fuzzy Zoeller in the 1983 Ryder Cup at Palm Beach Gardens.

Seve once described Sandy as "the greatest God-given talent in history. If everyone in the world was playing their best, Sandy would win, and I'd come second".

Lyle was a natural, but he eventually started to get bogged down with the swing teacher Jimmy Ballard. It was the worst thing he could have done because he got suckered into too many technical thoughts.

He wore this bra-type thing to keep his elbows together, then he would have a medicine ball between his knees. He got caught up in thinking too much. So much of that stuff is bullshit salesmanship but everyone is vulnerable because we all want to get better.

Players must stay strong and remain true to themselves. No one has ever attained perfection in golf because there are simply too many variables to contend with. You just can't go out there and shoot a 64 every day.

You might have a bad shoulder, a bad leg, the wind might be blowing at 40 mph, the ball will take a bad bounce on a links course. You've got to be in tune with reality to keep your finger on the pulse as to what makes you tick as an individual.

I never believed in all that technical mumbo-jumbo. When I was at my best, self-awareness was one of my strongest attributes. Lyle was one of the greatest-ever ball-strikers, and I don't know why he got caught up in overthinking about his swing.

You see the same thought processes with players who use long putters. The South African, Harold Henning, called them a "crutch" and he was right. You only use those things when you're not sure of yourself.

I should know; that's what happened to me when my game fell apart. Putting made me miserable and that's why I decided to retire. When you are mentally crippled by bad experiences after you've missed more than your share of short putts, you start second-guessing yourself, and the mind focuses on the outcome instead of the execution.

Everyone needs to stay in execution mode, especially when you've got the putter in your hand because a three-footer is just as crucial as a 300-yard drive.

Players go to the long putter due to anxiety. When you make that decision, it's a sign that a player is deeply unsure of what he is doing. The great Sam Snead once said, "Of all the hazards in golf, fear is the worst".

No player is going to announce to the world that he is not as good as he used to be. Sam Torrance holed that terrific, curling effort to win the

Ryder Cup at The Belfry in 1985. He did it with the short putter; it flowed for him; he was super confident.

Torrance, though, finished his career with the long putter. His good friend Ian Woosnam was the same, Sandy, too. It's a merry-go-round but the key word for all of them was fear.

When I won our PGA Championship at Hillside in 1982, Sam was marking Bernhard Langer's card. The likeable German, who was plagued by the yips, knocked one in from three inches at the last hole to get into the play-off.

Langer was putting cross-handed that year and Sam wasn't completely sure what had happened. Once we were all in the scorers' hut, he asked, "Did you hit that putt just the once?" Bernhard replied, "Yeah, just once." I was watching and I could vouch for that.

But it's another example of what can happen when you are gripped with fear. Bernhard has used so many putting methods down the years.

He's a remarkable man. How the hell he achieved what he did on the regular tour, and how he's broken all the records on the Seniors tour, defies belief.

He's what the Americans would call 'a phenom'. A man with amazing fortitude. Bernhard's also been using the long putter and he holes so many with that thing.

I used the long putter for a while but never won a tournament with it. The best I did was finish third. But when fear strikes a player, he is done for, especially among the true elite.

Once you achieve Major victories, there's a new expectation from the fans and the media. It places a much greater burden on you; the pressure begins to build, and before you know it, you're broken.

It's always real fun to get that first big win, and then the second one. The players who lift themselves up from the rest are those that win six, seven, eight, nine Majors — those who win 15 or 18 are in a different stratosphere altogether.

Another legend of the game, Bobby Jones, said it was all about the six inches between the ears. He stopped because he achieved all there was to achieve — he stopped because he had nowhere to go.

Byron Nelson retired at 34 because he said he had enough money to build the ranch he wanted. I know that was a lie. Tommy Bolt's wife told me that every night Byron's wife would be cleaning up after he had thrown up.

The expectation levels had increased to such an extent that he was making himself ill. You always need a mental place to go to find solace.

I always thought it was interesting that Tom Watson studied psychology at university. There could be no better subject to learn to prepare for a life as a top sportsman.

Testimonial from Bernard Gallacher (part 1)

Ryder Cup playing appearances: 1969, 1971, 1973, 1975, 1977, 1979, 1981, 1983

Ryder Cup captain: 1991, 1993, 1995

Mark James and Ken Brown made captain John Jacobs' job very difficult in 1979. They misbehaved, especially off the course, and John toyed with the idea of sending them both home.

In Ken's case, I put it down to youthful nerves. For Mark, it was down to bravado but there were nerves in there for him too. The pair of them just didn't get on with the rest of the side. They were like friends together, apart from the team.

It was pretty poor. We needed twelve people to be together to beat the Americans, but we only had ten. They were eventually banned from representing their countries; that's how serious it was.

The Ryder Cup is a big occasion and people sometimes act out of character in those situations. Mark and Ken weren't up to coping with the nerves of playing the Americans on their own soil, and they acted out of character.

My wife Lesley and Tony's wife Vivien confronted Mark at one point and told him, 'You have to start behaving because this is ridiculous.' He took it like a naughty schoolboy.

Mark and Ken were on the road on their own back then and, in some ways, that was the problem. They were both engaged to their future wives, but the British PGA didn't allow them to take their fiancées with them to the Ryder Cup.

That was a problem. It was draconian in those days because you couldn't take your partner if she wasn't your wife. It was a cost thing, it was run by the British PGA back then, rather than the European Tour, and executive director Colin Snape said we couldn't afford to take them.

It was ridiculous because the fact of the matter is, if it helps you play your best by having your partner with you, surely that's best for everyone. I think that was the root of the problem.

Most of us had our wives with us yet their fiancées were banned. I didn't agree with that policy at all, but I was just a player. Michael King was a member of that team as well and he said, 'Stuff it, I'm taking my partner'.

I always kept my head down and did whatever the captain told me, but other players needed more persuasion to play with this player or with that player.

The big difference in Tony's time as a captain was that it was a boys-together-in-the-team-room type of atmosphere. It was old fashioned until he arrived.

He broke down the barriers, and under him, the players could wear tee-shirts and trainers and no longer had to dress formally and make appearances in the dining room in the evening. That made it a much more relaxed atmosphere, more like it was week-by-week on the European Tour.

Chapter 9
1983 Matches

PGA NATIONAL GOLF CLUB, PALM BEACH GARDENS,
FLORIDA, OCT 14–16
Captains: T Jacklin (Europe), J Nicklaus (USA)

EUROPE: 13½, USA: 14½

Foursomes: Morning
B Gallacher & S Lyle lost to T Watson & B Crenshaw 5 & 4
N Faldo & B Langer beat L Wadkins & C Stadler 4 & 2
JM Canizares & S Torrance beat R Floyd & B Gilder 4 & 3
S Ballesteros & P Way lost to T Kite & C Peete 2 & 1
Fourballs: Afternoon
B Waites & K Brown beat G Morgan & F Zoeller 2 & 1
N Faldo & B Langer lost to T Watson & J Haas 2 & 1
S Ballesteros & P Way beat R Floyd & C Strange by 1 hole
S Torrance & I Woosnam halved with B Crenshaw & C Peete

Fourballs: Morning
B Waites & K Brown lost to L Wadkins & C Stadler by 1 hole
N Faldo & B Langer beat B Crenshaw & C Peete 4 & 2
S Ballesteros & P Way halved with G Morgan & J Haas
S Torrance & I Woosnam lost to T Watson & B Gilder 5 & 4

Foursomes: Afternoon
N Faldo & B Langer beat T Kite & R Floyd 3 & 2
S Torrance & JM Canizares lost to G Morgan & L Wadkins 7 & 5
S Ballesteros & P Way beat T Watson & B Gilder 2 & 1

B Waites & K Brown lost to J Haas & C Strange 3 & 2

Singles:
S Ballesteros halved with F Zoeller
N Faldo beat J Haas 2 & 1
B Langer beat G Morgan by 2 holes
G Brand Sr lost to B Gilder by 2 holes
S Lyle lost to B Crenshaw 3 & 1
B Waites lost to C Peete by 1 hole
P Way beat C Strange 2 & 1
S Torrance halved with T Kite
I Woosnam lost to C Stadler 3 & 2
JM Canizares halved with L Wadkins
K Brown beat R Floyd 4 & 3
B Gallacher lost to T Watson 2 & 1

You could have knocked me down with a feather when British PGA secretary Colin Snape and European Tour chief Ken Schofield approached me out of the blue at the Car Care Plan International at Sand Moor near Leeds in May 1983 and asked me to become Ryder Cup captain.

As far as I was concerned, I was done, finished with them altogether. I was peed off at John Jacobs, deeply hurt about being left out of his team as a player two years earlier in favour of Mark James, who behaved so badly in 1979, and being involved again was the furthest thought from my mind.

My immediate response to Snape and Schofield was, "Whoa, this is a shock — I'm not going to be able to give you an answer right now. I'll need to get back to you".

At that point, I really didn't care whether I took the job or not and, you might think this strange, but I couldn't have cared less about the Ryder Cup. I'd put the whole thing behind me entirely.

But as I began to absorb the reality of the captaincy offer, I thought this would be a great opportunity to put things right and make a real difference to the team's chances.

Travelling the same way as the Americans, who flew Concorde and had first-class of everything, was important for our mindset, and I believed a team room, something we never previously had, would be imperative.

I wanted food and beverage in there so that my players wouldn't need to go anywhere else. The idea of being left to our own devices in the evening wasn't conducive to creating team spirit.

That team room eventually became crucial to us, and all the players and wives embraced it. That was our inner sanctum — no officials, no fans, no media, it was just us together every night.

I gave my shopping list of demands to Snape and Schofield the next day and they agreed to all of them. PGA president Lord Derby was hovering around waiting for me to give my decision and, at that point, my main concern was Seve Ballesteros.

I went up to Lord Derby and asked him, "What about Seve?"

He replied, "You've accepted the job; he's your problem now."

As I mentioned earlier in this book, Seve was still seething about being omitted from the 1981 matches because of his long-running dispute with the Tour over the payment of appearance fees at regular tournaments.

I thought it was bizarre that he should be referred to as a "problem", and I made it my business to speak to Seve as quickly as possible. We soon arranged a breakfast meeting in the Prince of Wales Hotel at Birkdale, which was hosting The Open that season.

Seve spent the first half-hour venting about the Tour, and I had every sympathy. "I know, you don't have to tell ME," I told him. "As far as I'm concerned, they're a shower and not worth worrying about. But none of this matters now because they've given me carte blanche to do the job as I see fit — I want to make changes, and I can't do it without you."

100

He was hurt, his ego severely dented and he didn't think the Tour appreciated where he was coming from at all. Seve and I talked for an hour or more and eventually he said, "OK, Tony, I help you."

That was music to my ears, and I relayed the news to Snape and Schofield because at that stage we were meeting up pretty regularly getting everything ready for the matches.

The issue of appearance fees was something Schofield wouldn't budge on in his row with Seve and the Tour kept driving into a roadblock. To not utilise their most talented player to the benefit of the circuit was incompetence as far as I was concerned.

Seve doubled the gates, but, sure enough, just a few years later, there was a group of ten or twelve players who ended up getting appearance money.

Nick Faldo, Sandy Lyle, Ian Woosnam, Bernhard Langer, Colin Montgomerie and the like were all beneficiaries. Those players were rightly seen as drawcards, and they all attracted extra interest from the fans.

The sponsors, too, whether that was BMW, Volvo or whoever, always wanted the best players to feature at their tournaments because they were coughing up millions of pounds.

The Tour, however, never bothered to sit Seve down and ask him how he thought the two parties could create a win-win situation. The relationship was truly fractured.

So, with the Seve issue now sorted, I had less than four months to prepare. It was a fait accompli as far as the make-up of my team was concerned. I had no wild card picks, and my twelve players would all be automatic qualifiers from the top of the money list.

In another quirky twist of fate, it was Jack Nicklaus who was to be my opposite number as captain — a great friend and the guy who put sportsmanship ahead of personal glory by conceding that short putt to me back in the 1969 edition at Birkdale to leave the matches tied at 16-16.

I travelled to Palm Beach Gardens to meet Jack, to organise the hotel I wanted my players to use and to make sure the team room would be organised the way I had envisaged.

They were my priorities and beyond that it was a question of the British PGA and the European Tour taking care of our British Airways Concorde flights and sorting out the clothing. We arranged with Austin Reed from Savile Row in Mayfair to prepare proper outfits — the best blazers, shirts and cashmere sweaters.

Jack had a house no more than three miles from the PGA National Golf Club at Palm Beach and he agreed to host the traditional Gala Dinner on his front lawn.

TV rights were no big deal. Local ABC coverage was pretty much all there was.

Nowadays, every single shot is shown on Sky Sports. For those matches in 1983, such was the low-level interest after a succession of American drubbings, the BBC had just two 50-minute highlight programmes each day.

Seve, the linchpin of my team, was very much on board and happy to leave everything to me. Now and again, we would chat, and he would say, "Tony, you're a great captain; you do it."

Jack and I had been pals for a long time. I first met him at the 1966 World Cup in Japan when Peter Alliss and I faced him and Arnold Palmer. I used to go to his house for dinner, fish with him and generally goof around.

He was happy I had been chosen as captain. It had not been done before, but I told him I'd be handing out gifts to each of his players — personalised Waterford Crystal decanters.

It was important to underline the fact that the matches would be a friendly affair. Of course, both teams would want to win badly, but I was keen to ensure there would be no ill will.

I went on to do the same every year I was captain, giving the Americans a different piece of crystal with their names on and sending them all my best wishes.

Jack's card was marked, and he, in turn, got a company over there to make a reciprocal gesture. One year I remember my European team were all given a porcelain Ryder Cup.

I explained my thoughts to Jack about a team room and he decided to do the same for his guys. Our own personal caddies were also joining us for the first time and that had to be sorted out by the Tour and the PGA.

They had to get the caddies to Palm Beach Gardens and they had to be paid. The remuneration for my players and me was never really discussed. I don't remember ever receiving more than £2,000 in expenses. The honour of representing our tour and our respective countries was enough.

It was a new beginning, a new era for us all and we were really excited when Jack and his wife Barbara greeted us at the airport ahead of the matches.

For me, it was then all about making sure all the i's were dotted and the t's crossed. We gathered in the team room on the first night and straight away I told the players, "If you've got an ego, hang it on the hook outside the door because there's no room for egos in here.

"We're all equal and it falls on me to do what I've got to do, and it falls on you guys to do what you've got to do and together we're going to do all we can for the team. If you've ever got anything to say, come and say it, and I'll do the same to you."

We had two full days of practice. A lot of our players weren't playing on the US PGA Tour at that time and some of them weren't as familiar with the conditions as others.

It was really gratifying to see that the decision I'd made to create the team room, insisting we spent all our time together, was going down well. Everyone was very comfortable in there and the refreshments were spot-on.

One of the things I did, rightly or wrongly, was to tell the players they need not do any press conferences and that I would shoulder that particular burden. I wasn't swimming against the tide with that one because they just wanted to play, go back to the hotel for a shower and then chill in the team room.

I saw the press as part of my portfolio and the players were grateful. They could just relax away from the golf and be freed up as much as possible for the all-important action out on the course.

The powerhouse players in my team were all going to play 36 holes on the opening two days, so it was important to keep them fresh and focused. I talked to the caddies, who were a big part of the overall effort, and impressed on them the key roles they had to play in keeping their players fired up.

We went to Jack's house for the Gala Dinner. The gifts were exchanged out on his lawn, and it created a nice ambience. There was certainly a good feeling between the two sets of players ahead of the matches.

The whole experience that week was fantastic — the only downside was that we ended up getting beaten by the narrowest of margins after a nerve-wracking final day.

We had taken the lead on day one, up by 4½ points to 3½, and I felt the players were really responding to the way they were being treated, that all of a sudden, they no longer needed to view themselves as underdogs.

My team were now on an equal footing with the Americans, and nothing was going to make them feel inferior. Everything was first class, and our self-esteem was completely intact.

I could see my team were totally wrapped up in the matches, dedicated 100 per cent to the task. That's a life's work for a golf professional, getting in a Ryder Cup team, and it means so much to every individual.

Some players have even gone to the press and said they would rather get into a Ryder Cup side than win a Major. I'm not sure I'd have gone quite that far personally but it's true to say that every golfer on the European Tour aspires to play in the team event.

There was an interesting moment on the second day. Angel Gallardo, who was later to become the European Tour's vice-chairman, came up and told me Seve wasn't happy and that I needed to talk to his fellow Spaniard.

I caught up with the great man in the locker room as he was peeling off his shirt on another hot and steamy Florida day. "Are you OK?" I asked.

He said, "This boy, I have to tell him everything, which club to use, do this, do that. I feel like his father."

The twenty-year-old Paul Way was his partner in every one of the foursomes and fourballs. I never explained to Seve why I had decided to put the two of them together.

A lot of players were intimidated by Seve, but Paul wasn't. I could tell by his body language, he just got on with it. When we chatted in the locker room, I said, "But you are his father this week, Seve, in here," I explained, pointing to my heart.

"That's why you're with him. Is that a problem?"

Seve thought about it for a second before replying, "For me, Tony, it's no problem."

He and Paul then went out for the afternoon foursomes and beat Tom Watson and Bob Gilder 2 & 1.

Maybe Seve had said something to Angel that he wouldn't tell me, but we got it sorted. Assumption is the mother of all screw-ups, and I assumed he knew why he was playing with Paul. It was quite a shock to see that the penny hadn't dropped, and he hadn't seen it.

Paul played inspired golf with him, they took 2½ points out of four, and it was great to see them combine so well. The locker-room incident was just about the only negative moment I remember from that week.

It seems to have gone down in Ryder Cup folklore that I told Gordon Brand senior on the flight over that he wouldn't see any action until the singles.

I honestly don't remember saying it, but perhaps I did. Gordon and I never fell out, though. I never had any cross words with anyone at the PGA National.

There was great team unity. It was the week when confidence started to really build, and the bravado we had seen from previous European teams began to fade and turn into proper belief. It was the first time I could feel momentum being created in our team.

There was a definite change of mood. You could see that this was the way it was always supposed to be. The atmosphere among the players was fantastic and that all came from the feeling of togetherness created in the team room.

Everyone had everything they wanted in there and they were geed up, keyed up. There's a difference between negative nervous emotion and positive nervous emotion and my players couldn't wait to get out there — there was zero fear from them.

The hardest job I had was deciding who to leave out in the afternoon on the opening two days. I didn't have much time to prepare for that because the names had to be delivered before the morning matches had finished and it can be a tricky task working out who's in top form and who might be toiling a bit.

The two teams were locked together at 8-8 going into the singles. It had always been the done thing to put your best players at the end of the draw, but I didn't think there was much point in leaving my powerhouses to last because by that time the match could be over.

I completely flipped the names and put Seve out first against Masters champion Fuzzy Zoeller. I remember Jack being pretty shocked. "You can't do that!" he said.

That, for me, was one of the great things about the Ryder Cup. Putting the twelve names in the envelope and trying to outsmart your opposite number in the draw was one of the elements of the week I had most fun with.

One year I put my power in the middle of the order of play. I did everything I could in an effort to get to 14½ points before the Americans did. Points on the board were precious, far more important than getting everyone some action out on the course before the final-day singles.

I would not contemplate playing someone if he were incapable of putting a point on the board. That was the whole deal for me.

In the final match, with everything on the line and thunder and lightning crackling around us, Lanny Wadkins hit it stone dead with his approach to the 18th against Jose Maria Canizares and that proved the coup de grace for the Americans.

Lanny was a cocky little sod. I had known him a long time, and he was always as keen as mustard. He would refer to you as his golfing lunch, as if he could eat you up. He was never short of confidence.

Jack was in tears, and he described it as his "greatest-ever thrill". He bent down and kissed Wadkins' divot before proceeding to skip down the fairway with his players, who were so relieved to get across the line.

I did think over the last couple of hours that the momentum was with us. I dared to dream we could pull it off and it was gut-wrenching to fall just short.

What a last day it was, though. Seve, in the lead match, looked to be home and hosed when he went three up with seven to play. He then lost four holes in a row before producing a miracle shot at the last that none of us present will ever forget.

Unfortunately, there doesn't seem to be any TV footage of the moment but, in a fairway bunker 250 yards from the green and faced with a six-foot lip in front of him, Seve took out his three-wood and somehow managed to conjure a wonder shot to make the putting surface.

Jack called it "the greatest shot I ever saw".

Fuzzy said, "They say great golfers hit great shots but that one made me blink." Seve's caddie Nick De Paul was similarly awestruck because he had told his man to take a five-iron out of the sand.

It could so easily have been my team celebrating victory that day. Bernard Gallacher missed a three-footer on the 17th as he was squeezed out 2 & 1 by Tom Watson, Canizares looked like he might eke out a win against Wadkins, Seve held his big lead over Fuzzy.

We were crushed at the end, but Seve put it into perspective when all our heads were down. He punched his fist and said, "We must celebrate. This is like a victory for us because now we know we can win."

Faldo says now that it was the moment that we truly started to believe we could beat the Americans. When I got home, I went through the whole week in my mind, trying to assess if there was anything more I could have done, but I genuinely thought I got it all right.

In golf, you get beaten up a lot more times than you win; the statistics aren't even close from that point of view. But that was the turning point for us and, all of a sudden, we knew we could go into the next matches at The Belfry in 1985, believing we could win — that was undeniable.

I was disgusted that a lot of the British press who were out there at Palm Beach Gardens decided to go to Disney World on the final day; such was their interest in the outcome.

I guess they didn't have any copy to file because of the time difference, and they all came back with Mickey Mouse bags and stuff. That was disappointing because my guys had given their all out on the course.

The players and I licked our wounds for a week or two. We had two years to wait for our next chance but in that period, we got stronger. It was like a perfect storm really.

Everything was starting to come together. I had several world-class golfers, and, for The Belfry, I would have three selections at my disposal. The fact we managed to go so close with no captain's picks made our performance even more extraordinary.

It's crucial to be able to rest or hide players over the first two days. Exposing just eight of them is conducive to making close finishes — and we've had a ton of those in the last 30–40 years.

As much as anything else, that's what has pushed the Ryder Cup alongside soccer's World Cup and the Olympics Games as the three great showpiece occasions in world sport.

It's the greatest arena in golf now and it means everything to the European players. Christy O'Connor Junior didn't talk to me for four years after I left him out in 1985 and it's taken Philip Walton, his fellow Irishman, more than 30 years to forgive me for leaving him out in 1989.

It's true to say that it's a long way from Florida to Ireland but he had barely said three words to me before we met up in 2019 at the British Par-3 Championship that I host near Coventry.

Philip was upset for a long time that I overlooked him in favour of Christy in 1989. He may not have forgotten but I think he's now forgiven me.

Testimonial from Bernhard Langer

US Masters wins: 1985, 1993

Ryder Cup playing appearances: 1981, 1983, 1985, 1987, 1989, 1991, 1993, 1995, 1997, 2002

Ryder Cup captain: 2004

Tony Jacklin was still out on tour, a double Major winner, and the Tournament Committee of players felt he was the personality we needed in 1983.

We felt he would be a great captain because he was always very positive and had faith in us. He had beaten the Americans, he'd won the British Open in 1969, the US Open in 1970 and he knew we were as good as they were.

It was all about us believing that ourselves and about being treated properly. We used to turn up in rags while everything was first-class for the Americans. Our players were treated horribly, and we had basically lost before we'd even started.

But Tony changed all that. He had travelled the world, played in America, Europe, participated in numerous Ryder Cups and had been our most successful player for twelve or fourteen years.

He was a polished individual, a good speaker and we felt he had the leadership qualities that could unite us and instil the confidence we needed to beat the Americans.

Tony had also learned from previous captains in terms of what was good and what was bad. He had the ideas to make changes. He was the best guy to put forward — there was no one even close to him as a contender for the role. I felt he was the number one choice.

I probably didn't think he would shake it up the way he did, but it was his idea to fly Concorde, to get us new clothes, brand new bags and to get permission for us to take our own caddies.

Tony turned out to be excellent. He went far beyond what we had envisioned but he made us special and helped us perform better. He was always so positive. Even during the times when things didn't go quite the way we hoped, he would say, "You guys have the game, and you can compete against them".

He created a tremendous team spirit. I don't ever recall him saying something negative in any sense and I truly enjoyed playing under Tony. He was a great captain.

During the 1989 matches at The Belfry, I wasn't on top of my game. Something wasn't right with my swing, I wasn't hitting the ball the way I wanted, and I felt I should let Tony know.

I was almost in a mini-slump in a sense. I said to him, "I don't feel 100 per cent, and if anybody else on the team feels good about their game, you should give them a chance and I can go to the range and try to find what I'm missing."

That's the only time I ever said that in my Ryder Cup career. I felt I was playing fairly well in all the others, and I was always ready to play in all five matches if I had to.

Even if I was tired, I didn't care. You're so hyped up you don't care how tired you are. You can catch up on sleep the following week.

I recall Tony saying something like, "Look, you're one of my champions and I can't imagine leaving you out no matter how you're playing". I had complete respect for Tony and whatever he said, went, and I told him I'd go out there and try my best.

There were many Ryder Cups when I played five matches in three days and it's mentally exhausting, more than physically. Fourballs often take five hours or more while foursomes is a gruelling format because every shot counts — it's almost brutal.

It was always very tiring at a Ryder Cup with all the ceremonies, parties, dinners. There was much more going on than at a regular tournament.

Tony was always so approachable. If you had any doubts, he would reaffirm his belief in you and instil confidence. They were amazing qualities and he communicated very well with everybody.

He would say, "Are you okay with this?". He would always explain himself to the players and that was a great way to do the job. He said, "You're the best and you can beat anybody".

Tony had tremendous foresight. With flying Concorde, staying in nice hotels, having our own caddies, new clothes, new bags — all of a sudden, we looked like millionaires.

Those things made a big difference. He knew that and he forced them to spend the money and it paid great dividends.

The European Tour lives off the Ryder Cup now and if Tony hadn't had that foresight, who knows where the Ryder Cup would be now?

Photographs

Photography credit: Frank Christian

Present and correct. Nick Faldo, bottom left, looks on as my rival captain in 1983, Jack Nicklaus, and I exchange gifts before the matches at Palm Beach Gardens, Florida.

Ray Floyd was a steely competitor on the golf course but he seems tickled here by something I said.

Blue is the colour as my players join me for a team photo in 1983.

It's all smiles from me, my late wife, Vivien and British PGA president, Lord Derby.

Clockwise from top left: Now is not the time to take a backward step, TJ; with Bernard Gallacher and José Maria Canizares at The Belfry; Paul Way was just twenty-two when he played at the 1985 Ryder Cup, but showed maturity beyond his years; my pocket dynamo, Ian Woosnam, showing his passion.

A window to our world. Vivien and I keep an eye on band practice in 1985.

Paul Way, Sam Torrance and Bernhard Langer watch Seve spraying me with champagne on The Belfry roof after our epic victory in 1985

Doesn't the eighteenth hole at The Belfry look a pretty picture? The patriotic crowd was my thirteenth man that week.

The match that changed the history of the Ryder Cup. Craig Stadler shakes hands with Sandy Lyle after the American had missed a tiddler of a putt at the eighteenth in 1985. I think Bernhard Langer and I are still in a state of shock at his blunder.

Sharing a joke with Mark O'Meara, rival captain Lee Trevino and Curtis Strange at The Belfry.

Enjoying some downtime with my old pal, Jimmy Tarbuck.

Dressed up to the nines. Vivien, centre, with the European wives and partners in 1985.

A tough nut to crack. Captain Trevino, far left, with his United States team at The Belfry.

Clockwise from top left: Straining to get a better view at Muirfield Village; Woosnam shakes hands with Larry Mize after he and Faldo got the better of the American and his partner, Lanny Wadkins, on the first morning; urging on my boys from the sidelines; the incomparable Seve waves to fans.

Seve, right by my side as always, and I lead the team out ahead of the opening ceremony.

Opposing captain, Jack Nicklaus, with another formidable US team at his disposal at Muirfield Village.

Getting the powers-that-be to allow the players to use their regular caddies was one of my key demands when I agreed to take over as Europe's Ryder Cup captain.

The players that made history by delivering the first European victory on US soil in 1987.

To the victors the spoils. An extremely proud captain lifts the trophy in delight at the end of a memorable week.

Sharing a special moment with British PGA president, Lord Derby, and his PGA of America counterpart, James Ray.

No flagging now! The celebrations are in full flow for me and my players.

Putting a marker down. Seve on the way to victory over Curtis Strange in the final day singles matches.

A first for Astrid. My new wife appears to be paying particularly close attention to what I have to say back at The Belfry in 1989.

A perfect way to bow out. My fourth and final match as captain ends with us retaining the trophy in front of Denis Thatcher.

In the driving seat. My trusted lieutenant, Bernard Gallacher, is in charge of the buggy at The Belfry.

Worthy opponents. US captain, Ray Floyd, holding the trophy, and his team worked hard to secure a 14-14 tie in 1989.

Mellow in yellow. I was truly blessed to be leading another terrific group of players for my Ryder Cup swansong.

Astrid and I with US captain, Ray Floyd, and his wife, Maria.

Centre of attention. Astrid is joined by the European partners and by José Mariá Olazábal's mother, Julia, second right.

They were both urging their rival husbands on, but Astrid and Maria still developed a good rapport at The Belfry.

Lapping it up. Astrid and I enjoying the cheers and back-slaps from the fans in 1989.

Chapter 10
1985 Matches

THE BELFRY, SUTTON COLDFIELD, WEST MIDLANDS,
SEPTEMBER 13–15

Captains: T Jacklin (Europe), L Trevino (USA)

EUROPE: 16½, USA: 11½

Foursomes: Morning
S Ballesteros & M Pinero beat C Strange & M O'Meara 2 & 1
B Langer & N Faldo lost to C Peete & T Kite 3 & 2
S Lyle & K Brown lost to L Wadkins & R Floyd 4 & 3
H Clark & S Torrance lost to C Stadler & H Sutton 3 & 2

Fourballs: Afternoon
P Way & I Woosnam beat F Zoeller & H Green by 1 hole
S Ballesteros & M Pinero beat A North & P Jacobsen 2 & 1
B Langer & JM Canizares halved with C Stadler & H Sutton
S Torrance & H Clark lost to R Floyd & L Wadkins by 1 hole

Fourballs: Morning
S Torrance & H Clark beat A North & T Kite 2 & 1
P Way & I Woosnam beat H Green & F Zoeller 4 & 3
S Ballesteros & M Pinero lost to M O'Meara & L Wadkins 3 & 2
B Langer & S Lyle halved with C Stadler & C Strange

Foursomes: Afternoon
JM Canizares & J Rivero beat T Kite & C Peete 7 & 5

S Ballesteros & M Pinero beat C Stadler & H Sutton 5 & 4

P Way & I Woosnam lost to C Strange & P Jacobsen 4 & 2

B Langer & K Brown beat R Floyd & L Wadkins 3 & 2

Singles:

M Pinero beat L Wadkins 3 & 1

I Woosnam lost to C Stadler 2 & 1

P Way beat R Floyd by 2 holes

S Ballesteros halved with T Kite

S Lyle beat P Jacobsen 3 & 2

B Langer beat H Sutton 5 & 4

S Torrance beat A North by 1 hole

H Clark beat M O'Meara by 1 hole

N Faldo lost to H Green 3 & 1

J Rivero lost to C Peete by 1 hole

JM Canizares beat F Zoeller by 2 holes

K Brown lost to C Strange 4 & 2

Howard Clark told me about an incident that occurred before the start of the 1981 Ryder Cup at Walton Heath.

Apparently, Europe's John Jacobs had asked opposite skipper Dave Marr to go easy on his team. Howard said, "I remember saying to someone, 'Even our captain doesn't think we can win!'"

Well, massively buoyed by our terrific performance at PGA National in Florida two years earlier, my players assembled at The Belfry in 1985 and couldn't wait to have another crack at the Americans. Our mission? To lift the trophy for the first time in 28 years.

I'm often asked what gave me the most pleasure, the two Major victories or my Ryder Cup captaincies? Thank God I don't have to choose. That's all I can say.

I wouldn't give up my Majors for all the money in the world, but exactly the same goes for my Ryder Cup record. Captaining twelve players in a team event that overflows with passion and patriotism was far more fulfilling from an emotional point of view.

Playing golf is always a roller-coaster experience because, even for the elite, you lose far more often than you win. But you can multiply the emotional aspect several times over when it comes to having twelve players relying on you to say — and do — the right things.

You're having to keep everybody sweet in a Ryder Cup week, and the whole process is something that's very tough to explain. I tried to give a flavour of what it means at the start of this book.

The relationship that develops between the twelve players that gather together can be compared to the bond that exists between a man and a woman. It really is as strong as that, like being in the trenches together in a war, if you like — a feeling of team unity you rarely find in golf, which is normally such an individual sport.

We've seen so many times, with so many captains down the years, how much it means. Look at the tears that were streaming down European captain Jose Maria Olazabal's face after the staggering comeback that capped the Miracle of Medinah win in 2012.

We also saw the way Seve Ballesteros and Nick Faldo, two of our greatest-ever players, wept uncontrollably as they fell into each other's arms after Bernard Gallacher's side pulled off their victory at Oak Hill in 1995.

That's how it gets to you when you've given everything you've got all week and manage to get across the line at the end. We're all made of the same sort of stuff and none of us would be out there playing golf, punishing ourselves the way we do, unless we cared deeply.

As a captain, it's like being the Godfather, the head of the family. You don't want to let your kids down; you try to make sure they have everything they need; you wrap them in cotton wool, and it's about keeping them happy, safe and comfortable.

The caddies, too, are important, more so than when I was starting out in the 1960s. Back then, they would be little more than bag carriers and quite often, you would be bailing your bagman out of trouble.

You'd see them sleeping rough on the golf course at times; you might even get them out of a prison cell after an indiscretion. Nowadays, they're talking about setting up a Caddies' Hall of Fame.

Personally, I wouldn't go that far, but the brotherhood between a player and his bagman in the modern game is clear for everyone to see.

Another key element of my role as captain at The Belfry in 1985 was to make sure the caddies were involved in the whole process. I talked to them on the first tee to underline the fact that it was their job to keep their guys calm.

I used to say, "Remember he's going to be nervous; I know you are as well, but you've got to help each other out." You cannot be afraid to be upfront with them — the caddies were integral to what we were trying to achieve.

The jitters can get to us all in a high-pressure situation like that. When I won The Open at Lytham in 1969, I remember walking down the second fairway and Willie Hilton, my caddie, felt so nervous he couldn't speak.

I had to give him a reality check, a little pep talk. "Willie," I said, "you're the only guy out here I can speak to, so snap out of it." That was enough to get his mind back on the task and we ploughed on.

Caddies can make errors of judgement — they're human too, but some players rely on them more than others. The pair have to be best friends and that's the kind of relationship you see out on tour much more these days.

It was also important to work closely with the greenkeeping staff at The Belfry. It was my right to set up the course the way I wanted. I made sure there was no long rough around the greens and that the putting surfaces weren't going to get too quick and favour the Americans.

We didn't want Lee Trevino's men being able to hit the flop shots around the greens that they're so good at. The Bermuda grass you often see in the States is two inches long, the ball sits up and the American players can get great control by sliding the club underneath it.

I didn't want the fairways narrowed either at The Belfry, which was a very young course. Our officials wanted to take it there in 1981 as well but I advised them against doing that, and they opted to play the matches on the outskirts of London at Walton Heath instead.

The Belfry is the home of the British PGA. The brewers Whitbread owned it back in 1985 and they gave the PGA, who didn't have much money, free office space.

If the PGA had managed to get their own way, we would have played every home Ryder Cup at The Belfry for the last 30-40 years.

Thankfully, though, we've been able to pay due respect to those players from Continental Europe who have made such an outstanding impact on the matches by taking it to Spain in 1997 and to France in 2018.

The Brabazon was a very immature layout in 1985, the best example of what happens when you are operating on a shoestring budget. Both the courses at The Belfry were built on the cheap for £350,000 and it probably ended up costing them more to renovate than it did to create in the first place.

Looking back, it is hard to say what the going rate would have been in those days but, by way of example, the Concession Golf Club in Florida I co-designed with Jack Nicklaus that opened in 2006 cost $10 million to build.

The idea of building a top-class golf course for £350,000 is laughable. Peter Alliss and Dave Thomas were the architects at The Belfry, and they had an impossible task. It was like trying to make a silk purse out of a sow's ear.

But it has to be said that the greenkeeping staff did a helluva fertilising job and, because there was so much clay in the soil, they also had to drill the fairways to fill them with sand. All in all, though, we were good to go on the opening day.

We didn't get off to a great start, losing the morning foursomes 3-1. I felt I had to change things and I left Faldo, Sandy Lyle and Ken Brown out of the afternoon fourballs.

There were no real dramas from any of them. Not everyone's going to be on top form so, as a captain, you have to busy yourself keeping a close watch on each of your twelve players.

Sometimes you have to go on instinct and take a chance or two with your selections. I often say it's like flying by the seat of your pants, but you must be prepared to go with the flow and that's what I tried to do.

We narrowed the deficit to a solitary point by the end of the day and it was the two Spaniards — Seve and Manuel Pinero — who were at the heart of our push for glory.

Manuel is one of my favourite people in golf. He's a lovely guy and, back in 1985, he was such a tenacious individual in match play.

That's why a captain must be allowed to make some picks. You wouldn't back Manuel in medal play, but he was a terrier in the Ryder Cup.

I saw less of Manuel that week than I did the other players. His father had accompanied him to The Belfry and Manuel felt he needed to take care of him, kind of chaperone his dad, who spoke no English.

The other great quality he possessed was that he wasn't overawed by Seve. Jose Rivero, who was also in that 1985 team, was intimidated by his fellow Spaniard but Manuel was inspired by him.

Manuel was almost born to play in the Ryder Cup. He was like a dog snapping at your ankles; he was so determined, and you just couldn't shake him off if you were up against him.

Seve, being the great man that he was, recognised his influence. There was a moment when the crowd were going wild as the pair were walking across the bridge on the 18th hole and Seve grabbed Manuel's arm and lifted it to the skies to make sure the adulation was shared.

Seve was like a one-man army. I had total commitment from him. He did whatever it took — barring cheating because we obviously weren't going there — but we needed to have this passionate resolve to get it done and he and I never left a stone unturned.

Nothing else mattered than knocking the Americans off their perch. We had been beaten often enough. He was so focused. He was awesome and as strong off the course as he was on it — and in that period he was the finest golfer in the world.

His influence was there for all to see. I was no longer captain at Kiawah Island in 1991 but I helped Bernard Gallacher behind the scenes, and it was there I had to tell David Gilford that he was the player we had to withdraw from the line-up because of American Steve Pate's injury.

That was the worst thing I had to do at a Ryder Cup. I did it as a favour for Bernard. David was a lovely guy, very low key and perhaps in awe of some of his teammates.

At the start of that week at Kiawah, I was sitting next to Seve and asked him to go and give Gilford a rub on the shoulders and tell him how good he thought he was as a player.

Seve went over, massaged David's shoulders and said, "I see you're swinging so good now, well done". That sort of thing was no problem for the great man. He exuded charisma.

Fellow Spaniard Sergio Garcia has a much better all-round game, more ability as a shot-maker, but in terms of raw courage there was no one better in golf than Seve.

Sergio has been a brilliant performer in the Ryder Cup, no doubt about that, but he is such a talent, probably the best in the world from tee-to-green for the last twenty years, and he really should have more Major victories to show for his outstanding attributes.

Winston Churchill famously declared that it's courage that counts. If you don't have that, you're always stepping into the unknown. You must have that steely-eyed determination to get the job done.

Seve was absolutely the most courageous golfer who played under me. Some of the putts he holed were amazing and his miraculous recoveries from around the green defied belief.

He got nervous with his long game, became too excited and started swinging too fast. He often went awry off the tee but didn't try to control that element of his game because he was happy enough to stage those brilliant recoveries — that was why he was so interesting to watch.

Seve and I shared a car at one point as we travelled to get our clubs fixed in 1979, not long after his so-called 'car park champion' exploits helped him win The Open for the first time at Lytham.

I tried to explain that it's a much easier game from the fairway and that he should try and work on slowing his swing down, especially at the all-important time when he was coming down the stretch at a tournament.

He said, "But you don't understand, Tony." He was just that way, with his Spanish flair and passion. He never, ever lost his amazing touch around the greens and he was always supremely confident.

Some people believe he hated the Americans but how can you hate Jack Nicklaus, Arnold Palmer and guys like that? Seve never dwelled on that with me but for him, the Ryder Cup represented a marvellous opportunity.

He liked beating them because they had the best of everything, and we didn't. Whatever European country you're from, whether it's Henrik Stenson in Sweden, Bernhard Langer in Germany, Thomas Bjorn in Denmark, as a junior, you never get the same opportunities as the Americans do.

They have much better courses, a much better climate and a great college system. The Ryder Cup is a chance for our guys to shine and to show that, even though we might not have the money they've got across the other side of the pond, we can still play.

The second day at The Belfry featured the turning point of the match — perhaps even the turning point in the long history of the competition — as Craig Stadler missed an absolute tiddler from two feet on the last green.

Stadler and Curtis Strange were leading Lyle and Langer and it was a real shock to see what transpired. His blunder helped our guys salvage a precious half-point and suddenly the momentum seemed to swing heavily in our favour.

I was sat by the green for Stadler's miss and I was left stunned. I wanted to win, of course I did, but I didn't want to win at the expense of an opponent making a fool of himself.

Seve was so excited at that point. He could smell blood and some of the other players told me that he jumped up and fell off the back of his chair in the team room, straight into Ken Brown's lap as he watched it all unfold on television.

The players said Seve was so intense as he sat there, staring at the screen just a couple of feet away, almost willing Stadler to miss. You could say his failure to hole that putt changed the whole course of Ryder

Cup history, bearing in mind how many times Europe has won since that incident.

I really couldn't believe what happened. He was just long enough away for the putt not to be a 'gimme', and he completely missed the hole on the left side. It didn't even lip out.

I'd rather one of my guys hole a 30-footer to get a point or a half-point than see someone fall on his face the way Stadler did.

When I got back in the team room to join the rest of the players, Seve still hadn't calmed down. I have to confess feeling a little sorry for Stadler but there was no pity whatsoever from my chief lieutenant.

Sam Torrance said there was bedlam in the team room when that match was halved. It was just what our side needed because we got an immediate injection of confidence. It was such a powerful, positive moment, no doubt about it.

The Belfry was humming too, the players were feeding off the excitement of the galleries. There was so much anticipation in the air, and we took advantage big time by winning the afternoon foursomes 3-1 to open up a 9-7 lead ahead of the singles.

We notched up some big wins, too — Canizares and Rivero smashed Tom Kite and Calvin Peete 7 & 5, Seve and Pinero swept the unfortunate Stadler and Hal Sutton aside 5 & 4 while Langer and Brown eased past Wadkins and Ray Floyd 3 & 2.

The Americans were clearly worried because half their side was still out there practising in the dark at the end of the day. Our team room, though, was rocking again.

When the draw came out and Pinero discovered he would be taking on Wadkins in the first singles on the last day, he jumped four feet in the air.

Wadkins was the cockiest member of the American team. As I mentioned in the previous chapter, he looked at opponents on the first tee as if to say, "I eat people like you for lunch".

Pinero, though, took care of him 3 & 1. He kicked Wadkins' ass and his win had a tremendous galvanising effect on his teammates. It made him our top points scorer that week with four and it was exactly what I was looking for when I put him out first.

There were some top guys in our team. Young Paul Way was always a positive influence, constantly smiling and, like Seve, exuding self-belief. It was a surprise he only went on to win three times on the European Tour in his career.

Langer was another great team man and an outstanding professional. I've often said that you could pair him with anybody in the Ryder Cup. It didn't bother him a jot who the hell he was asked to play alongside.

Soccer is first, second, third and fourth in terms of sporting popularity in our country — the others don't even go close. And it's at the Ryder Cup that I see why the British so love the team aspect, it's tribal to them, bi-partisan, and you fall on one side or the other — there's no grey area.

The crowd were our ace in the hole at The Belfry and the place erupted when Sam Torrance holed the winning putt at the last. What an unforgettable moment that was — it will stay with me for as long as I live.

It doesn't get any better than closing it out the way he did. Sam never managed to win one of golf's big prizes so that was like his Major victory. It was pure theatre and, of course, the party started straight away as we all began knocking back the champagne on the 18th green.

We eventually returned to the on-site hotel, climbed through a window and the team and I continued the celebrations on the roof of the pro shop. The fizzy stuff was still flowing, I was on Sam Torrance's shoulders and Seve was spraying me with champagne.

I recall Langer saying, "I'm twenty-eight and it's been twenty-eight years since the Americans have been beaten — that's a very long time."

I replied, "It's been a long time for me too because I was thirteen when my dad took me to Lindrick for the last win."

We finally went into the clubhouse for the traditional post-match dinner but that's always a bit of a yawn for me because one team tends to be down.

The players had had a skinful by then. We all had our smart Austin Reed suits on, and I was later dragged down to the swimming pool where Torrance and Woosnam gave me a drenching. I waddled back down the corridor feeling less than chuffed.

I was cold, saturated and my suit was ruined. I could've done without that experience, and I decided to leave the players to it because I then went back to my room, put my dressing gown on and helped myself to a whisky.

And that was fine by me. If I had my way, I might have celebrated like that in the first place. Everyone celebrates differently — Sam and Woosie like to have a singsong for instance. I was done for by then and I didn't need to be thrown in the pool; I know that much!

I never said this before the 1985 matches because I wanted to be fully focused on the task ahead but, in the aftermath, victory tasted a little sweeter because we achieved it against Trevino.

I had to take it very much in the solar plexus from him in The Open at Muirfield in 1972, where I was beaten into third place, and I was a bit disappointed he never came over to congratulate me when victory was clinched at The Belfry.

I would have thought so much more of him if he had. Trevino doesn't like losing, although it has to be said that probably stems from the fact that he spent more time winning than losing in his playing career.

Of course, we all react differently, but if you can't look your opponent in the eye at the end of it all and say, "well done", then we're all wasting our time. I think it's important to do the right thing at those moments.

Everyone was so excited at our victory that it led to a bizarre conclusion to the 12th and final singles match between Ken Brown, who was a notoriously slow player and generally brought up the rear so as not to hold the rest up, and Curtis Strange.

The celebrations and partying was already underway elsewhere as the pair arrived on a deserted 16th tee with no galleries for company.

They discovered that the tee blocks had been taken and a bemused Ken asked tour official John Paramor, "Where do we play from?"

John settled things pretty speedily by sticking the point of his umbrella deep into the turf and replying, "Go from there.".

Then, when the players made their way towards the green, they noticed the flag had also been removed. John again used his umbrella to good effect, placing it in the hole to allow Curtis to wrap up a 4 & 2 win.

There were a couple of downsides to our team's victory. Faldo was out of form that week. He was going through a divorce at the time, so it was a difficult period for him.

He only played in two sessions and lost on both occasions, but he still partied with the rest at the end. Nick is a bit different, I suppose, but he and I have always got on very well and we regularly speak to this day.

Some of the Americans had a bit of a whinge. They complained about the crowd's hostility, opponents walking on their putting lines, their wives being booed and even about match officials being against them.

Trevino, to his credit, refused to join in, and he called them cry-babies. I felt I had put one over on him, though. I remember telling the press at the start of that week that I believed strongly in getting my pairings right, that it was important to get the best out of them by putting them together with people they can gel with.

The US captain didn't agree. He said it didn't matter who played with who on his team. He had the supreme confidence that the Americans always seemed to possess, that sort of, 'we'll go and kick butt attitude' that was so typical of past teams.

The crowd gave us great support and it made the hair stand up on the back of the neck when you stood on the first tee on the final day and all you could see was an ocean of home fans.

We were also a different team in 1985. My players had proved two years earlier that they could compete with the Americans, and we arrived at The Belfry overflowing with self-belief.

That's the way it sometimes happens in elite sport. You often have to go close before ultimately breaking through. It's a very fine line at the highest level, but our team unity was there for all to see, and the majority performed to the very best of their abilities.

Testimonial from Ian Woosnam

US Masters win: 1991

Ryder Cup playing appearances: 1983, 1985, 1987, 1989, 1991, 1993, 1995, 1997

Ryder Cup captain: 2006

If it wasn't for Tony, the Ryder Cup might have died a death back in the day. The British PGA and the European Tour did a great job listening to how Tony wanted things run.

He was a player I looked up to when I was a youngster. Following in his footsteps was an inspiration for any young player back then.

Seve Ballesteros had played with young Paul Way in 1983. I then teamed up with Paul in 1985. I don't know why he put us together, it was Tony's idea, but it worked well.

We were two feisty players. We gelled well and won two of our three matches as a pair. It was a little bit of a surprise after Paul and Seve had performed excellently two years earlier but when I played under Tony, I was happy to play with anyone. I was the sort of person who got on with anybody.

It was a bit of a shock when he paired me up with Nick Faldo in 1987 and 1989. But Nick was always so consistent and never made many mistakes, so that allowed me to go ahead and play really aggressive golf, especially in the fourballs.

Tony always made you feel like you were an essential part of the team. You weren't just on the sidelines. He would ask how you felt, and he made you feel really at home. That was the great thing about his captaincy; he took on board your advice as well.

He was the best at man-management and paved the way for future captains to follow the same style over the next thirty years. I played under a few captains and there were times when people didn't feel part of the team.

We were fortunate to have a great group of players coming through in Tony's era, but he had the foresight to make it all happen the way it did.

Chapter 11
1987 Matches

MUIRFIELD VILLAGE, COLUMBUS, OHIO,
SEPTEMBER 25–27
Captains: T Jacklin (Europe), J Nicklaus (USA)

EUROPE: 15, USA: 13

Foursomes: Morning

S Torrance & H Clark lost to C Strange & T Kite 4 & 2

K Brown & B Langer lost to H Sutton & D Pohl 2 & 1

N Faldo & I Woosnam beat L Wadkins & L Mize by 2 holes

S Ballesteros & JM Olazabal beat L Nelson & P Stewart by 1 hole

Fourballs: Afternoon

G Brand Jr & J Rivero beat B Crenshaw & S Simpson 3 & 2

S Lyle & B Langer beat A Bean & M Calcavecchia by 1 hole

N Faldo & I Woosnam beat H Sutton & D Pohl 2 & 1

S Ballesteros & JM Olazabal beat C Strange & T Kite 2 & 1

Foursomes: Morning

J Rivero & G Brand Jr lost to C Strange & T Kite 3 & 1

N Faldo & I Woosnam halved with H Sutton & L Mize

S Lyle & B Langer beat L Wadkins & L Nelson 2 & 1

S Ballesteros & JM Olazabal beat B Crenshaw & P Stewart by 1 hole

Fourballs: Afternoon

N Faldo & I Woosnam beat C Strange & T Kite 5 & 4

E Darcy & G Brand Jr lost to A Bean & P Stewart 3 & 2

S Ballesteros & JM Olazabal lost to H Sutton & L Mize 2 & 1

146

S Lyle & B Langer beat L Wadkins & L Nelson by 1 hole

Singles:
I Woosnam lost to A Bean by 1 hole
H Clark beat D Pohl by 1 hole
S Torrance halved with L Mize
N Faldo lost to M Calcavecchia by 1 hole
JM Olazabal lost to P Stewart by 2 holes
E Darcy beat B Crenshaw by 1 hole
J Rivero lost to S Simpson 2 & 1
B Langer halved with L Nelson
S Lyle lost to T Kite 3 & 2
S Ballesteros beat C Strange 2 & 1
G Brand Jr halved with H Sutton
K Brown lost to L Wadkins 3 & 2

That week has to go down as the best of my golfing life but, for two separate reasons, it could all have turned out so differently.

Firstly, and scarcely believable as it sounds now, there had been a move to replace superstars like Seve Ballesteros, Nick Faldo and Bernhard Langer in my European team with a group of unknown club professionals.

Long before the European Tour was conceived in the 1970s, the British PGA were the trustees of the Ryder Cup prize donated by Samuel Ryder and the figure of one of their most famous members, Abe Mitchell, stands on top of the gold trophy.

Everything seemed to change after we won for the first time in twenty-eight years at The Belfry in 1985. It was a case of 'ka-ching, ka-ching' because the PGA now wanted more of the proceeds generated by the event.

It got to the point where they threatened to send a team of British club pros to defend the trophy at Muirfield Village — it was that ridiculous.

The PGA demanded a 50-50 share of the proceeds. I argued for a 60-40 split in favour of the European Tour, and that was when PGA president Lord Derby turned around and said, "You've upset me."

I said that I was sorry, but there's no way the PGA should get 50 per cent. In fact, deep down, I thought they were entitled to less than 40.

The players, who of course are all European Tour members, never got involved in the arguments but when I think of the Ryder Cup, that discussion always comes to mind. My team were out there at The Belfry in 1985, giving their all and putting their careers on the line.

In the end we settled on an acceptable 60-40 split but I'm not sure Lord Derby ever forgave me. I'd never been a club pro; I was an assistant in my younger days. I was really the first player to make a full-time living on our Tour and I was fully reliant on the prize money I won.

Players like Dave Thomas, Dai Rees and Max Faulkner all had club jobs in the off season. From the mid-sixties, I would travel to South Africa to compete in the winter and then play in the UK in the summer.

I was always on the side of my players and the European Tour and, as captain, I felt it was right to speak up on their behalf. In the end, I was thrilled we resolved the matter in our favour.

It became very clear at the time that it was all about money for the PGA because they could see how the Ryder Cup had suddenly taken off.

There were so many European players that had come on stream. It wouldn't have been fair to the likes of Seve, Langer and later, Henrik Stenson, not to benefit from the competition.

The Tour gave me carte blanche to do what I wanted as captain. They gave me the power, I insisted on a 60-40 split, and the Tour backed me. But it also meant I got the blame from Lord Derby and the club pros.

I played in seven Ryder Cups as a player and money never entered my head. It was the same when I was captain. I can't recall talking about money to any of my team during my time in charge.

I think we got about £2,000 in expenses back then and for the players, it was all about the matches.

Nowadays, the Ryder Cup is probably worth £100 million in total revenue. It's a massive event. It's grown to be so unbelievably successful, and everyone is so passionate about it.

People say it's currently worth £1 million in spin-offs for the captain, and director Guy Kinnings recently told me the Ryder Cup brand is now bigger than that of the European Tour. That's what it has become — it's that huge.

The second reason why the week could have turned sour for me was that I would have played no part in the event if the European Tour had bowed to the demands of the PGA of America.

I wasn't surprised in the least to hear three or four months after our victory at The Belfry that the Americans requested a change of format. They always want to win, win, win — coming second doesn't mean a jot to them.

That's why they never change the format of the Presidents Cup. That's a competition they always win, and that attitude underpins everything they do in sport, in life.

After years and years of being battered, we had suddenly found a schedule of matches that made it easier for us to compete and now they wanted to shuffle the cards.

Money was driving the Americans on, too. They wanted to stretch the Ryder Cup from three to four days, knowing full well that would lead to extra revenue coming in.

When I was told of their wish to change the format, I was adamant and unambiguous with my response. I told the European Tour, "I'm gone if you agree to that, I'll resign as captain."

The Tour, to their credit, backed me 100 per cent. The PGA of America had dollar signs in front of their eyes, but we stood firm. We gave them an outright 'no' and the issue was never raised in my company again.

Let's be clear here. The PGA of America would not have cared less whether I was captain or not. To them, it was simply a way of trying to load the dice in their favour.

Some people don't realise that the US PGA Tour have little to do with the Ryder Cup, it's the PGA of America's baby and they are always responsible for picking their captain.

More often than not back then a player would need to win the US PGA Championship in order to be chosen as skipper. I remember feeling badly for Larry Nelson, for instance, when Tom Kite got the job in 1997.

Larry had won the US Open and US PGA earlier in his career and 1997 should have been his year. But Kite got the job that time and it was clear Larry was never going to get it going forward. He's a great guy and received a really raw deal.

David Duval had the PGA of America in his sights, too, when he won The Open at Lytham in 2001. He was pretty forceful when it came to asking for more money for the US Ryder Cup team.

His thinking was, 'why should the PGA of America be grabbing all the spoils while it's the Tour players who are doing all the work?'. It wasn't long after that they agreed to give the players more cash.

Money was never an issue in our camp, and I was never involved in any meetings with the PGA of America. I always went through European Tour chief executive Ken Schofield or his eventual successor George O'Grady.

George, when he worked under Ken, was always very involved in the Ryder Cup and I remember asking him after I captained the team for the fourth time in 1989, "How long am I supposed to do this?"

He turned around and said, "As long as you want, Tony."

Four times was enough, though, and I've never regretted my decision to stand down when I did. It would have been self-indulgent to do more, plus there were elements of the job I was getting uncomfortable with.

I loved the golf side of things; choosing my wild-card picks, the pairings and the camaraderie with the players was second to none. But away from the course, it was getting trickier.

Players were starting to want to bring their kids along, for example. I never even dreamed of doing that when I was a player, and it was something I didn't agree with.

Going back to the 1987 matches at Muirfield Village, we were all taken good care of by John Hines, the club's manager, while Jack and Barbara Nicklaus were also fantastic hosts.

John was a really nice guy. The two of us struck up a good friendship, and I was sad to hear of his death on his 74th birthday a few years ago. He was diagnosed with cirrhosis of the liver — even though he didn't drink.

When he came over to London, I used to tell him which Chinese restaurants to go to. He was so grateful to me for pointing out the best places to visit.

I had a deal with the Mayfair Hotel, which was the bees-knees in those days. I used to do golf days and such like for them and, in return, I was able to stay there whenever I was in the capital.

The first thing I think about when I recall the 1987 matches is that we were playing in Jack's backyard at Muirfield Village — the venue that had hosted his Memorial Tournament for years.

When we arrived, a press man stuck a microphone under my nose and demanded a prediction. "We'll win," I said.

He asked, "How can you say that with such confidence?"

My reply was, "Because... because... because."

Nick Faldo was walking behind the pair of us, and he started to babble the words "because... because... because".

The vast bulk of the galleries were Memorial patrons, and they weren't like the partisan crowds that had caused some of the American players to complain at The Belfry two years earlier.

On the first day, both teams received polite applause; there was no special atmosphere for the home team. It was like the local decorum you see when the Memorial comes around every year.

My two powerhouse pairings — Ballesteros and Olazabal and Faldo and Woosnam — set the tone for their performances that week with victories in the morning foursomes.

Then, remarkably, we hammered the Americans 4-0 in the afternoon fourballs — the first time they had ever been on the receiving end of a clean sweep in any Ryder Cup session — and it was to happen once more on the first day fourballs in 1989.

Seve and Ollie won again, as did Nick and Woosy, who were absolutely on fire. They gelled brilliantly as they stormed to the turn in 29 shots, leaving Hal Sutton and Dan Pohl struggling to live with them.

It was 6–2 to us at the end of the day. I guess Jack thought he needed to do something drastic at that stage. He ordered thousands of little Stars and Stripes flags and told the PGA of America to distribute them among the crowd for the second day.

Jack urged the fans to be more patriotic and to make more noise, but it was a bit like shutting the gate after the horse had bolted. We were already operating at a steady gallop in our team room.

The Americans wanted the crowd to be more vociferous, but they just wouldn't go there. The strategy would probably have worked in Boston or New York — it's not tough getting the New Yorkers excited about their own.

I recall Faldo, who had won The Open at Muirfield a couple of months earlier, calling the second day gathering 'rent-a-crowd'. He thought it was embarrassing to have 25,000 Americans suddenly waving Stars and Stripes flags.

It had no real effect on the matches because my guys were on a mission to conquer Everest by winning in America for the first time. At the start of the week, everyone thought the super-fast greens would work in the home team's favour, but it turned out to be completely the opposite.

Lanny Wadkins, typically, tried to stir it up at the start of the week by pointing out that 1985 Masters champion Bernhard Langer and Seve, a four-time Major winner at that stage, had not won in the States for two years and that they both really needed to play more in the US.

I had so many world-class players in my team by then and they lapped it all up. Faldo and Woosnam maintained their unbeaten sequence by halving their morning foursomes against Hal Sutton and 1987 Masters champion Larry Mize.

I'll never forget the last hole as Seve and Ollie faced Ben Crenshaw and Payne Stewart. Needing to get down in two from 10 feet to clinch victory, Seve sent a curling effort racing six or seven feet past the hole.

"Uh-oh, that could be a mistake," I thought as I watched from the side of the green. But Ollie showed nerves of steel and rammed the return putt straight into the middle of the hole.

Seve's relief was palpable. Grinning from ear to ear, he strode up to his fellow Spaniard and gave him a great big bear hug, something I repeated seconds later. What a combination they were turning out to be — three victories from three matches in their first Ryder Cup together.

They had such an indomitable spirit and a feeling of togetherness. Little wonder they would go on to prove one of the greatest partnerships in the history of the competition.

Seve and Ollie suffered a rare defeat in the afternoon fourballs, going down 2 & 1 to Sutton and Mize, but Faldo and Woosnam made it 3½ points from four matches by romping to a 5 & 4 victory over Strange and Kite.

Theirs was a bit of an unlikely pairing, and I remember Woosie in particular being somewhat surprised when I announced they would be playing together, but they complemented one another so well that week.

Woosie was an up-and-at-'em, attacking type of player, while Faldo could be relied upon to be rock solid. It's probably fair to say they weren't exactly bosom buddies off the course, but on it, they dovetailed perfectly.

It was a leftfield pairing, and it worked. It was an instinctive decision to play them together. All I did was watch everyone as closely as I could, trying to gauge body language, and I wasn't afraid to act on a hunch.

Armed with a huge lead at 10–5 going into the singles, the pundits thought it was all over. I never entertained those sorts of thoughts — I'd been in the game too long.

You never think it's all wrapped up. The Americans have produced several phenomenal last-day performances, and I knew golf far too well to believe that the Fat Lady was clearing her throat just yet.

I certainly felt comfortable with the lead, but you always have to wait and see what happens. That guy Murphy is never far away. Murphy's Law can take care of a helluva lot — I can vouch for that following my experiences with Trevino in The Open at Muirfield in 1972.

It's the easiest thing to say and the hardest thing to do but you just have to stay in the present. You're on a slippery slope to nowhere if you allow your mind to start wandering.

That's the case with all sports, the central thing to being a winner. You have to stay in the moment and avoid going to that make-believe land of the If-ahs, the Would-ahs, the Could-ahs and the Should-ahs.

You might think you deserve it, but sport has nothing to do with deserving. It's about staying in the now and remaining in your own bubble until you cross the finish line.

Often, as a sportsman, the more you want something, the more difficult it is to stay in the present. I strayed for a moment when I won The Open at Lytham in 1969.

I was going down the 14th hole and I said to myself, "I wonder in an hour from now what it's going to be like". Instantly, I physically slapped myself around the face.

No one knew, my caddie didn't, the fans didn't, but I told myself, "Stop that right now! You can't go there".

Going into that final day at Muirfield Village in 1987, all it needed was an early momentum surge from the Americans to put us under pressure, and, sure enough, that's exactly what happened.

We came close to cocking it up when the score got to 12–11 in our favour but an incident in the Eamonn Darcy-Ben Crenshaw match would prove pivotal — comparable perhaps to Craig Stadler missing his tiddler of a putt at The Belfry two years earlier.

Crenshaw, furious with his touch on the greens, slammed his putter into the turf at the sixth hole and broke it. Forced to putt with a one-iron the rest of the way, the odds were very firmly on a Darcy victory.

Now, Eamonn had never won a full Ryder Cup point in 10 previous attempts, so if he was ever going to break his duck, this was the moment.

Crenshaw did wonders to stay with him while using a makeshift putter, but I was ecstatic when my man rolled in a treacherous, downhill six-footer to pull it off at the 18th.

It was an extremely difficult putt on those slick greens. The ball could have rolled 10 or 12 feet past the hole if he had missed. A proud Eamonn punched the air in delight when it disappeared into the cup.

It was then left to Seve to secure overall victory for us by defeating Strange, who would go on to win the US Open in successive years in 1988 and 1989, by a 2 & 1 margin.

It was time to start another party. We had great team unity again that year and everyone was whooping and hollering as twinkle-toes Olazabal began to show off his dance moves on the green.

We were grateful to the couple of thousand European fans who had travelled over and backed us so well all week and Lord Derby spoke highly of us in his speech later.

He said to our supporters, "You'll always be able to say you were here for this historic moment."

I thought that very profound, right on the nose — it was a great thing to tell our merry bunch of golf enthusiasts.

I was quite emotional when it came to my turn to make a speech. I took it upon myself to introduce every player on each team and to thank them for entertaining everyone so much.

It was only right to start with Jack Nicklaus. I went all the way down the line, asking for applause for every individual before I suddenly had a mental block when I got to one of the American players.

Faldo was right behind me, and he whispered, "It's Payne Stewart, Payne Stewart." I think I was already deaf at that stage but eventually, I got his name out.

Payne showed he had taken it all in good heart because when I got back to my hotel room later that night, under my door was a picture of him with the words, "Best wishes, Payne Stewart".

It was a very special week, in fact, I think it was more special than The Belfry had been. It was beyond even that; it was simply the ultimate. There's only one first time and we did it at Muirfield Village.

We went to see our fans in the tented village to thank them for their efforts and ended up having a few beers and celebrating with them. I felt so strongly about the contribution our supporters had made that, when we got back to the hotel, I felt we should do even more.

I called all the guys together and said, "Look, I know you won't want to do this, but we've got to go and thank the fans again."

'Oh, bloody hell,' was the collective response, but our cars were waiting out at the front, and we drove over to where the supporters were staying.

When we got there, all we could hear was the noise of knives and forks clinking on crockery. We walked in with the Ryder Cup trophy and the place absolutely erupted.

I told the players that we only needed to spend a short while there to show our appreciation. I recall saying to Seve after ten or fifteen minutes, "OK, we've done our duty, shall we go back now?"

He said, "No, no, we want to stay. We're happy here." That moment, and Seve's reply, sticks out in my mind and we continued partying with the fans for quite some time.

My players had been in command all week. Previously, it was always our team that wilted under pressure near the end of matches, but an awful lot of American balls finished up in the stream at the 18th on the final day, showing that it was now happening the other way. Jack's guys now knew my players were supremely confident.

A different home captain might have struggled to recover from the stigma of losing in America for the first time. Not Jack, though. He was untouchable after all the Major victories he had amassed, including his sensational victory at the Masters the year before.

Being beaten on home soil was never going to harm him too much. He had enjoyed such a remarkable career until then, that it would just go down as a blip on his radar screen.

Jack agreed that the 18th hole had proved pivotal to our 15–13 victory, with Crenshaw, Mize and Pohl all succumbing there. "Our guys are not as tough as the Europeans," I recall him saying, and there was no argument about that.

For us, it seemed like we had gone through a seamless transition from 1983 to 1985 and then to 1987. We hit the ground running from the start and simply picked up where we left off at The Belfry.

I went with instinct a lot of the time when it came to the decision-making process. You can't necessarily always explain the logic of everything you do — you haven't got time either.

It's often all about just going with your hunches and, I've said this so many times in the past; you pray a lot. You go to bed at night and pray that you get everything right.

A lot goes on in a captain's mind during a Ryder Cup week and, more than anything, you've got to be prepared to make snap decisions, live with them and move on.

Look at the idea to put the six-foot-two Faldo and the five-foot-four Woosie together. I don't really know how that one evolved; maybe it was a little and large thing. I was just looking for a spark, some magic.

I always liked to keep the Spanish players together if I could, for reasons of patriotism and the simple fact that they spoke the same language.

Seve and Ollie were an inspirational partnership. Not only did they push each other on, but they also had the same galvanising effect on the other ten players in our team.

That was undoubtedly the best week of my life. When it comes down to captaining a Ryder Cup team, there's so much more on the line than when it's just you and your performance.

Winning the 1969 Open and the 1970 US Open were obviously wonderful personal accomplishments but there's so much more attached to things when you're leading a team of twelve men.

Hillary and Tenzing famously did it in 1953 and beating the Americans in their own backyard for the first time 34 years later was our version of climbing Everest.

I refused to take anything for granted that week. I wrote everything down, but I never dwelt on things too much. At the end of the day, everyone has to play at some point, and you never know for sure what order of play the other captain will decide on.

You can't ever guarantee a certain player going up against another from the opposition. That's another stupid thing they do in the Presidents Cup. They do that for television, and it's thought up by people who think they are making a movie.

The drama and spice of the draw, not knowing who is going to play against who, is an integral part of the Ryder Cup. It's the old adage; if it ain't broke, why try and fix it?

Clearly, I'm biased but you cannot compare the two competitions.

While I think about it, virtually every US president in the last half a century has been a golfer. What a pity we in Britain can't say the same thing for our prime ministers.

When Seve's winning putt went in, I was elated and so relieved. A lot of emotion was wrapped up in those three days, dreaming we would get the job done. Nicklaus was such a great sport in defeat, too.

There was some talk after the matches about making Muirfield Village the permanent home of the Ryder Cup in America. But Jack had already hosted 11 Memorial Tournaments there and that was his bag. It was that event that was front and centre in his mind and the idea didn't get off first base.

Another element of our victory that made it so special was the fact that not everybody in my team was a superstar. We also had the likes of Ken Brown, Jose Rivero, Gordon Brand Junior and Howard Clark.

Howard featured in three of my four matches as captain, and I had a lot of time for him. He was a really gutsy player and a very good exponent of match-play golf. Faced with an all-important four-foot putt, you could always rely on him to knock it in.

There were no over-the-top celebrations from me at the end of it all — I didn't normally go in for those and I certainly didn't go near any swimming pools this time around.

I had a whisky or two to toast our win, sat down and allowed it all to sink in. There were a few sore heads on Monday morning, and I can safely say that mine wasn't one of them.

We flew back on Concorde and there was a great reception for us when we landed at Heathrow Airport — a lot of people turned up to welcome us home, and it was a grand occasion.

Our victory had gone down well with the public; it was clear to see. It also did wonders for the European Tour, gave our rank-and-file a lot of momentum and served to inspire many young, aspiring golfers — what more could you ask?

Testimonial from Jack Nicklaus

Open wins: 1966, 1970, 1978
US Masters wins: 1963, 1965, 1966, 1972, 1975, 1986
US Open wins: 1962, 1967, 1972, 1980
US PGA Championship wins: 1963, 1971, 1973, 1975, 1980
Ryder Cup playing appearances: 1969, 1971, 1973, 1975, 1977, 1981
Ryder Cup captain: 1983, 1987

Tony Jacklin and I have a friendship that began six decades ago as competitors on the golf course and continues to this day.

Tony is, without question, one of the most accomplished and influential British golfers of our era, and perhaps in the history of the game. He is certainly a figure of legendary status in golf.

In addition to setting so many records during the height of his playing career, Tony was a hero throughout the United Kingdom with his wins in both the United States and British Opens.

His influence was also felt in the leadership role he took with such international events as the Ryder Cup, becoming the winningest captain in history and the first to claim victory on US soil.

Most importantly, Tony has left his mark on the game, international sport and his country through his conduct and generosity. He is a gentleman of strong character who is highly respected among his peers.

He is a dedicated family man and a great ambassador who represents Britain and the United Kingdom with great pride.

Chapter 12
1988: A Tumultuous Year

There was no Ryder Cup in 1988, but it was a real shocker of a year for me.

My wife Vivien died suddenly in April at the age of forty-four after having a brain haemorrhage at the wheel while driving near our home in Spain.

It came completely out of the blue. Our three kids, Bradley, Warren and Tina, were teenagers at the time and our whole world was turned upside down.

I was playing golf at Valderrama with 007 Sean Connery, my racing driver friend John Fitzpatrick — the European Grand Tour champion in 1972 — and Japanese property developer Shun Tezuka.

My good pal and former Ryder Cup playing partner Dave Thomas rushed to the course to give me the tragic news. He had found Vivien at the scene and heard her last breath after opening the car door.

As you can imagine, I was in a complete daze. In Spain, funerals are normally held within twenty-four hours, and suddenly, there was police everywhere, making enquiries and ensuring nothing untoward had occurred.

Everything was happening so quickly. Nick Faldo and European Tour chief Ken Schofield travelled over, as did my parents. Sean Connery and John Fitzpatrick organised the church service and Viv was buried in San Roque the very next day.

It was so, so difficult to come to terms with it all. After a few days, everyone went back to their normal routines; the kids were at school again, and it became a lonely old world for me for a while.

It's impossible to understand the gut-wrenching heartbreak of losing a spouse until it happens to you. I lost the will to live for a spell and contemplated doing something terrible. I was diving into the whisky every night and I could easily have drunk myself to death.

Six weeks after Viv died, I travelled to London to play in the Four Stars Pro-Celebrity tournament at Moor Park and it was there that I met a young waitress called Donna.

I never asked her age, but it turned out that she was only sixteen. As I'm sure you can imagine, my head was still all over the place, and she eventually came home to Spain to stay with me for a few days.

At the same time, a friend and neighbour of mine told me about a Norwegian lady travelling to the area to stay with her sister and brother-in-law. He thought I ought to meet her, so I went around.

Astrid was in the swimming pool when I arrived. Her sister introduced us, and it was pretty much love at first sight. That was that as far as Donna was concerned.

She was in tears when I told her our brief liaison was over, and it was at that point that I put her on a plane in Gibraltar. She flew home and walked straight into the London offices of *The Sun* newspaper to spill the beans.

In no time at all, our relationship was being plastered all over the front pages and dozens of British press guys started to camp outside my front door in Spain.

Meantime, Astrid and I were getting to know each other a little better. We were going on picnics and stuff but, with all the fuss going on around us, we decided to clear off one night.

The two of us escaped into the country to a hotel near Malaga called La Bobadilla — somewhere the King of Spain used to stay. We spent about a week there, and Dave Thomas was one of the few people who had my number.

My neighbour Peter Mead, who was chairman of the London advertising agency Abbott Mead Vickers, also knew where Astrid and I were. We kept calling to see if it was all-clear to return, but the answer was always 'no — it's still on the front pages'.

Then, after a week or so of anonymity, Astrid was in the pool when I went up and told her it was time to leave because the former Manchester United football star George Best had stepped up to the plate.

George said he'd known Donna for quite some time and, to cut a long story short, it seemed as though I was now off the hook as far as the tabloids were concerned.

As quick as a flash, the publicity turned positive; it was now a 'Jacklin finds love' type of story. Astrid and I were hounded for a while, but we just started to get on with everyday life. She had been divorced five years earlier and had two young kids in tow - Anna May and AJ.

Astrid was living in Miami when we met, but I told her to stay with me and that I'd take responsibility for the kids too. It was a whirlwind time, as I'm sure you can imagine, and we decided to get married in the first week of January.

The British press got hold of the story, so we stole a march on them and tied the knot on December 29 at the same church in Gibraltar where John Lennon and Yoko Ono got married.

If truth be told, the deep feelings of grief were still hanging over me. Viv and I had been happily married for twenty-two years but Astrid seemed to understand and gave me the time and space I needed to slowly come to terms with everything.

I was also heavily involved in setting up a golf facility in San Roque at that point. It was owned by Shun Tezuka, it was his money behind it, and it was due to be called The Tony Jacklin Club.

By the start of 1989, the Ryder Cup in September was beginning to take up more and more of my thinking. I would need Astrid's help at The Belfry, and it was important to start introducing her to the game and prepare her for what was to come.

Dave Thomas said I shouldn't involve my new bride, that it had always been a Viv and me thing. But you have to move forward in life and that's what I tried to do.

The two of us were making plans but we continued to have all sorts of dramas. Our young son Sean was born in 1992 but, prior to that, Astrid had gone through three unfortunate miscarriages.

In the summer of 1990, we decided to leave Spain — which obviously held so many poignant memories of Viv — and move to a big eleven-bedroom hunting lodge in Scotland.

Our new home was in a small village near Lanark, and we fell in love with the place. Country life suited us down to the ground, but it wasn't long before I was drowning financially.

I just wasn't making enough money to sustain living there; I was closing in on my fiftieth birthday in July 1994 and decided the only way to escape from the mess was to start playing again — on the lucrative Seniors Tour for the over-fifties in America.

The thing I was most accomplished at doing was playing golf and I had the bug again. I wanted to get as fit as I could and prepare properly, and that meant living in the States.

Astrid adored Scotland but it simply wasn't possible to stay there. I was doing TV commentary and a few bits and pieces here and there, but I didn't have any management representation at that time — I was making three and it cost four; it was a situation that couldn't last.

Back in the Eighties, I was advised to become a 'Lloyd's Name'. The Lloyd's of London insurance market operates as a society of corporate and individual members. The essence of it is that you underwrite twice as much as your net worth.

Despite my successes on and off the golf course, I've never come close to being a millionaire and, in terms of Lloyd's, I would show, say £100,000 and they would underwrite £200,000.

But some so-called 'Names' were exposed to massive claims when Lloyd's lost about £8 billion between 1988 and 1992 chiefly due to asbestos and pollution policies from the US.

'Names' were traditionally anonymous. Aristocracy and big banking families had dominated, but a new kind of 'Name' began coming to the fore in the Seventies such as boxer Henry Cooper, tennis player Virginia Wade and Formula One star James Hunt.

Politicians including Edward Heath, Michael Howard and Jeffrey Archer were also involved, as were businessmen Rocco Forte and Robert

Maxwell. Media reports said each 'Name' lost an average of £287,000 in five years, but some lost a lot more.

I left IMG in 1983 — ironically the first year of my Ryder Cup captaincy — telling the big chief Mark McCormack there was no point being with them because no deals were coming in for me.

Being a Ryder Cup captain meant nothing financially at that stage. The matches were such a one-sided affair, we were always getting beaten and there was precious little commercial interest in the competition.

It took ages to extricate myself from IMG and I owed back taxes at a time when the higher rate in Britain was extremely punitive.

I was advised to take out a stop-loss Lloyd's policy to protect losses of £18,000 or more in any year. I thought I had a pretty good spread, and the policy would have limited any losses.

But the rules changed during Margaret Thatcher's time as Prime Minister and by 1995-96 I was wiped clean out.

When we made the decision in 1993 to go to America to prepare for my new career on the Seniors Tour, we stayed with Jack and Barbara Nicklaus in Florida for three months. I then got a five-year deal to represent the developers of the PGA National — venue of the 1983 Ryder Cup.

Tom Crow at Cobra Golf gave me a contract from January 1994, six months before I was eligible to play on the Seniors Tour. He was a great guy, and Astrid and I could live off that money for a while.

Jack's organisation was also helping to look after me. I thought golf course design would be a lucrative option, but he had four sons who came before me in that regard.

I was lucky enough to win the First of America Classic in Grand Rapids, Michigan, on my fourth appearance as a senior, but just as I was starting to get going, the Lloyd's of London thing came to a head, and I needed to borrow money to pay back what I owed.

I had to find $350,000 at that point, and I was rescued by my son-in-law and by a good friend in Chicago. It was a bloody tough time, and it took years to pay them back.

165

There were 35 or 36 tournaments on the Seniors Tour in those days and the Americans were still anti-foreigners. When the rules were put together, they did everything possible to keep us out.

None of the international money I had made earlier in my career was allowed to count because it was solely about what you had earned in America. I was relying on exemptions to get into events and, had I not won in Michigan, I would have struggled to make a living.

The rules and regulations were set by the likes of Gardner Dickinson, Bob Goalby and Don January and you could rest assured those guys were doing their best to keep me out, just as they had tried to do 25 years earlier when I started out in America.

I played about 35 tournaments from July 1994 to July 1995. It was exciting at the beginning to see new places and enjoy fresh experiences, but I overdid the golf — it was way too much.

Lee Trevino and Dave Stockton were chalking up the most wins and they never took time off either. It was almost like they didn't have homes to go to and the rich pickings on tour were a financial bonanza for us all.

I just wanted to play 14 or 15 tournaments a year at my own pace but that proved impossible. If you opted to take a week off, it was like tossing money away.

I won again at the Franklin Quest Championship in Park City, Utah in September 1995. The first prize most weeks was $97,500 - my finances were still stretched, and I seemed to be constantly under pressure.

In the end, it was turning into a replica of what happened to me on the regular tour twenty years earlier. After two or three years, I told Astrid, "I can't do this anymore — it just isn't any fun."

The financial side was demoralising. I wasn't exempt despite my two Major wins because they counted for nothing. Suddenly, though, American Bill Rogers — who won the Claret Jug at Sandwich in 1981 — got to 50, he wasn't exempt and the powers-that-be now made The Open an exempt category.

It wasn't going to happen for me but, of course, they did it for him. I was later inducted into the Hall of Fame in 2002. Apart from winning those two senior events, I hadn't done anything noteworthy in golf since 1990.

Being in the Hall makes you exempt from qualifying on the Seniors Tour so they could have done that for me much, much earlier and saved me a lot of worry and aggravation.

The odds always seemed to be stacked against the 'Limey'. Colin Montgomerie never won a Major, but he was an IMG client, they got him in the Hall and, bingo, that was like a passport to untold riches as a senior for him.

Astrid and I scraped by one way or another. I got the idea to co-design with Jack Nicklaus the Concession Club where I live in Bradenton.

Looking back, it was the most traumatic year for me but apart from that terribly sad period, I've not got too many things to complain about when I look at the overall picture.

It's been a helluva life, I've travelled everywhere I ever wanted to go, met some great people — kings, queens, princes and princesses — and have always enjoyed fabulous support from my family. That's something money certainly can't buy.

Chapter 13
1989 Matches

THE BELFRY, SUTTON COLDFIELD, WEST MIDLANDS,
SEPTEMBER 22–24

Captains: T Jacklin (Europe), R Floyd (USA)

EUROPE: 14, USA: 14

Foursomes: Morning

N Faldo & I Woosnam halved with T Kite & C Strange

H Clark & M James lost to L Wadkins & P Stewart by 1 hole

S Ballesteros & JM Olazabal halved with T Watson & C Beck

B Langer & R Rafferty lost to M Calcavecchia & K Green 2 & 1

Fourballs: Afternoon

S Torrance & G Brand Jr beat C Strange & P Azinger by 1 hole

H Clark & M James beat F Couples & L Wadkins 3 & 2

N Faldo & I Woosnam beat M Calcavecchia & M McCumber 2 up

S Ballesteros & JM Olazabal beat T Watson & M O'Meara 6 & 5

Foursomes: Morning

I Woosnam & N Faldo beat L Wadkins & P Stewart 3 & 2

G Brand Jr & S Torrance lost to C Beck & P Azinger 4 & 2

C O'Connor Jr & R Rafferty lost to M Calcavecchia & K Green 3 & 2

S Ballesteros & JM Olazabal beat T Kite & C Strange by 1 hole

Fourballs: Afternoon

N Faldo & I Woosnam lost to C Beck & P Azinger 2 & 1

B Langer & JM Canizares lost to T Kite & M McCumber 2 & 1

H Clark & M James beat P Stewart & C Strange by 1 hole

S Ballesteros & JM Olazabal beat M Calcavecchia & K Green 4 & 2

Singles:

S Ballesteros lost to P Azinger by 1 hole

B Langer lost to C Beck 3 & 1

JM Olazabal beat P Stewart by 1 hole

R Rafferty beat M Calcavecchia by 1 hole

H Clark lost to T Kite 8 & 7

M James beat M O'Meara 3 & 2

C O'Connor Jr beat F Couples by 1 hole

JM Canizares beat K Green by 1 hole

G Brand Jr lost to M McCumber by 1 hole

S Torrance lost to T Watson 3 & 1

N Faldo lost to L Wadkins by 1 hole

I Woosnam lost to C Strange by 2 holes

Nine months after getting married, it was Astrid's job to look after the wives and partners of both teams during the Ryder Cup at The Belfry.

Raymond Floyd was the US captain that year. I was concerned for Astrid ahead of it all as I felt like I had chucked her in at the deep end. But it was an exciting time for her, and she got on like a house on fire with his wife Maria and they became good friends.

Everything went like a well-oiled machine and my task was to work out how to keep up the momentum that the players and I had created in 1983, 1985 and 1987.

Sandy Lyle was always an integral member of my teams. He had picked up his second Major victory in the 1988 Masters at Augusta, but he didn't want to play at The Belfry.

I begged him, I said, "Come on, I need you."

However, he was adamant. "I'm just not up to it," was his reply. He felt he wasn't playing well enough to be picked, and, it has to be said, the

Ryder Cup isn't the type of arena where you want to make a fool of yourself.

On the plus side, I could put Christy O'Connor Junior in the team, and the reaction I got was difficult to believe. He hadn't spoken to me for four years since I'd preferred Jose Rivero to him for the matches at The Belfry in 1985.

The only time Christy had talked to me in the intervening years was when Viv died. He came up and told me how sorry he was before turning around and walking away.

He was over the moon at being recalled in 1989 for his first appearance in fourteen years. I recall Chris De Burgh being at the Gala Dinner that year and giving us a few renditions of his 'Lady in Red' number one hit. Christy got up with him at one point for a duet and played the spoons on his knees.

The Americans wanted revenge for the two previous editions, and one of their players, Mark Calcavecchia, spoke for a lot of their side when he said he would prefer victory in the Ryder Cup to winning a Major.

Calcavecchia, who had won The Open at Troon earlier in the year, tried to stir it up. He said the European Tour wasn't a patch on the PGA Tour and that some of his fellow American professionals could do worse than join our circuit if they needed an injection of confidence.

Floyd had also claimed at the Gala Dinner that he had "the best twelve golfers in the world". Interest levels back in the States had soared to such an extent that the matches would be the first in Europe to be televised live in America.

None of that bothered my 'one-man army' and team linchpin Seve Ballesteros, who was as fired up for the 1989 matches as he had been for the previous three. "It's no secret I love to hammer the Americans and that's what I intend to do," was his retort.

We didn't make the best of starts and had to settle for two half-points from the opening foursomes as we trailed 3–1 — but the afternoon fourballs were a totally different story.

Seve and Olazabal, my dynamic duo, led the way by overwhelming Tom Watson and Mark O'Meara 6 & 5. Seve, in particular, was red hot as he finished with a staggering eagle-birdie-birdie-birdie sequence. Ollie famously remarked, "When he gets his Porsche going, not even Saint Peter in heaven can stop him."

Meanwhile, Faldo and Woosnam were as hungry as they were at Muirfield Village two years earlier as they took care of Calcavecchia and Mark McCumber by two holes.

There were victories too for Sam Torrance and Gordon Brand Junior, and the Yorkshire pair of Mark James and Howard Clark as we swept the board 4–0 in the fourballs. Perhaps it was no surprise that Floyd copped some flak at the end of the day for changing all his morning pairings.

Honours were even on the second day and that meant we got to the singles holding a 9–7 lead. My overriding memory of that whole Ryder Cup was the fact my star names came unstuck on the final afternoon and we were rescued by our unsung heroes.

Seve, Faldo, Woosie and Langer didn't pick up a half-point between them, but Christy Junior came up trumps when I needed him and Jose Maria Canizares clinched the singles victory that meant we retained the trophy when he sank a two-footer at the last after his opponent, Ken Green, had three-putted.

My go-to man in the first match was Seve, and, lo and behold, he drew the equally combustible Paul Azinger, who was making his debut for the Americans.

Paul is now a Florida neighbour of mine in Bradenton and graciously agreed to write the foreword to this book, but I didn't know him back then.

When I was walking out in the grand procession during the opening ceremony, I reached out and said, "Have a good week."

He looked shocked, as if to say, "Why is the captain of the opposition team offering me his hand?"

Paul's a tough cookie, he has never worried about having a 'go' if the mind takes him and he reminds me of Bernard Gallacher in that sense.

Azinger caused plenty of raised eyebrows when he claimed his team were going for a 12–0 clean sweep in the singles. He and Seve clashed on the 13th hole, and it wouldn't be for the last time in Ryder Cup combat.

The Spaniard glared as he twice told his opponent's caddie, Billy Poore, to move back. "That was great," Azinger said to his bagman. "You showed him we're not backing down… but don't do it again, okay? I don't want him mad at us."

Both players went on to find water at the last hole. There was another dispute about where exactly one of the balls had crossed the hazard but, ultimately, it was the American who walked off the green with a one-up victory.

Langer lost the second match 3 & 1 to Chip Beck but Ollie won the last two holes to scramble his way past US PGA champion Payne Stewart, who also found the drink on 18.

Payne was the real deal, no doubt. He was an extrovert, didn't mind wearing a bit of flashy gear, the plus-twos and the over-the-top socks but, boy, he could play. He was great for golf and a good sport. It was a very sad day when he died in a plane crash ten years later.

Ronan Rafferty was handed the onerous duty of taking on Calcavecchia. My young Northern Irish rookie, the only debutant in our team, was a fine player and I had a chat with him on the first tee.

"Ronan," I said, "you haven't won yet this week but you're too good not to come out of this with a point. Go and get the job done."

I don't know whether my gee-up had an impact or not, but Calcavecchia found water twice at the last and that was another point we could add to our tally.

I still believe passionately that a lot of the influential media guys don't realise there's a massive chasm between medal-play and match play. At professional level, anyone can beat anyone in match play.

It's a totally different mindset and you can take chances in that arena. You can struggle, post a nine or a ten, but only one hole is lost, and you can continue firing at the pins if you're an aggressive player.

Seve and Azinger are good examples. Two tough cookies who were never concerned with playing protective golf or with looking after their scores.

The media can be critical when it comes to wild-card selections by a captain, but I always thought of the match play element.

Manuel Pinero is another case in point: he was so much better in head-to-head encounters than he was at medal-play. Howard Clark was another, someone who holed out on the greens so well under pressure.

The chief reason behind the current Ryder Cup format is to make it a close-run affair and, as a captain, you need to be able to leave players out on the first two days if they are having a bad time.

You have to know that your twelve best available soldiers are available to you. My last words to the European Tour when I stepped down as captain were, "Never change the format because it makes it the fantastic event it has become."

After Rafferty's win, I caught up with Christy Junior on the 17th hole. I was kneeling down on the edge of the green, watching Fred Couples, his opponent, closely, and I could see his hands were shaking.

Couples missed his five-foot putt, and I ran up to Christy on the 18th tee. "You've got him now; he's gone," I said, "all you need is a nice drive up here on to the fairway, and you're there."

My man did exactly that while Fred pulled his tee shot 20 yards left. He was a big hitter, much longer than Christy, and it was his length that saved him. Otherwise, he'd have found the water.

We started walking down the fairway and I knew how important that match was to us. I urged Christy on with, "One more good swing for Ireland." He took out his two-iron and hit one of the best shots of his life as he drilled it superbly on to the green.

Fred then fell apart, missing the green with his eight-iron. He succumbed in the heat of the moment, as any of us can, and was in tears, but it was monumental for Europe to pick up a point from that match.

When Canizares prevailed against Green, it was all over. It had been another remarkably exciting match, nip and tuck all the way through, and my guys brought home the bacon.

Ray Floyd did a good job with his team. The Americans were all very competitive, just like their captain always had been as a player, but we hung on by the skin of our teeth.

"Once again, we couldn't get past the 18th hole," said the US skipper, "our guys kept hitting it in the water there, and you just cannot do that against world-class players."

I was a bit like Olazabal would go on to be after the Miracle of Medinah in 2012, very emotional. Most of the front pages of the next day's broadsheet newspapers featured a photo of me cradling the trophy like a baby - the evocative picture that is on the front of this book.

It was another great moment to savour and the perfect time to bring down the curtain on a wealth of Ryder Cup memories.

The two sets of players never really mixed after the matches in those days. The tendency was to make a beeline for the team room at the end; that was our sanctuary away from the media, the officials. It was just me, my players and all the wives and partners.

My four matches as captain had been such a lot of fun and it was time to go. I didn't want to be greedy and do it again in 1991. I loved doing the pairings and handling all the golf issues, but it was getting a bit tedious off the course in terms of politics.

The players, for instance, wanted to start bringing their kids to the matches, asking for adjoining rooms. There was some back-and-forth and I didn't have much patience in those discussions. My kids might have turned up for the final day when I was a player, but they were never there all week.

I was also very conscious of not outstaying my welcome. Margaret Thatcher was in power, and it was round about that time that some of her cabinet colleagues started to rebel, and the longest-serving British prime minister of the 20th century ended up losing her job.

Ironically, it was her husband Denis who presented me with the trophy in 1989. He was a keen golfer and a good sort; he certainly liked a gin and tonic or three. He told me a woman approached him that week to say, "I hear you've got a drinking problem."

His response was, "You've got it wrong — it's not a problem at all!"

174

When Viv was alive, we were invited to a banquet at Windsor Castle to mark a state visit by the King of Spain - more of that later in the book. In that environment, Maggie and Denis were just commoners.

The four of us stood talking together at cocktail hour before dinner, all peasants together if you like. I always found Maggie very pleasant company, and Denis was a good guy.

I didn't want to be stabbed in the back the way she eventually was. As far as the Ryder Cup was concerned, there was nothing more to achieve from a personal standpoint.

Even though George O'Grady of the European Tour said it was my job as long as I wanted it, I thought it would be self-indulgent to stay on. I had no regrets; I always wanted to leave the whole European environment in a better state than when I arrived — and I think I managed to do just that.

Testimonial from Bernard Gallacher (part 2)

Ryder Cup playing appearances: 1969, 1971, 1973, 1975, 1977, 1979, 1981, 1983

Ryder Cup captain: 1991, 1993, 1995

I'm a big fan of Tony's — in fact, I'm not sure there's a bigger fan out there than me.

He should have received a knighthood a long time ago. In today's world, he would have got one just for winning The Open.

Back in 1969, we had been waiting eighteen years since Max Faulkner's win at Royal Portrush for a British victory. There was a lot of pressure on home players in the late sixties and Tony's triumph was an inspiration to many.

Then, a year later he won the US Open by seven shots to prove he was a very high-level golfer. He was British through-and-through, and he broke down barriers as a player, and later as a captain in the Ryder Cup.

He is one of the main reasons the European Tour has been so successful since it was formed in 1972 and I am amazed he hasn't been knighted. His achievement in winning The Open, US Open and his inspirational Ryder Cup captaincy is as worthy as the 1966 World Cup win was for the footballers.

I don't know why the country leaves it so late for some people. We did that with Sir Henry Cotton because he received his knighthood posthumously. Maybe it's because golf isn't that popular, I don't know.

The Americans recognised Tony's achievements, he's a Hall of Famer over there. He was an inspiration for the likes of Sir Nick Faldo and the late, great Seve Ballesteros admired him so much.

Bob Charles is a Sir of course and he's a great guy, a great golfer, and I've got lots of respect for him, but Tony's done more for British golf than Bob has done for New Zealand — I just don't understand it.

Tony's been a tireless worker for British golf, and he was a visionary as a Ryder Cup leader. Before his time, captains were quite staid, quite formal.

Everything was very regulated; the players were expected to turn up in the dining room every evening and stuff like that.

Tony, though, was ahead of his time. He wanted to make it all so much more relaxed, more informal. He wanted a team room-type of atmosphere, with everyone else kept out.

But the biggest single thing he did was to get Seve on board in 1983. He had a very close relationship with Seve, who didn't play in the Ryder Cup two years earlier because of his acrimonious fallout with the European Tour.

It looked like he had played his last Ryder Cup and Tony persuaded him to get on board, to get behind the project, and they became great friends.

Tony was very close to all the top players — Faldo, Langer, Woosnam and Lyle — and he made them believe we could beat the Americans.

He was always very positive and, of course, his captaincy coincided with a big change in world golf with Europeans like Seve, Langer, Faldo, Woosnam and Jose Maria Olazabal all doing so well.

Tony made it a real knees-up type of atmosphere in the locker room and the players bought into it. I had played in every Ryder Cup from 1969 to 1983 and the first one I missed was 1985, the year of our historic victory.

One of the reasons I didn't make the team was because I was concentrating on my job as club professional at Wentworth. The European Tour was getting more expansive at that time, becoming more like a world tour.

I had to make up my mind what I wanted to do and tried to split my time between tour golf and Wentworth — hence I didn't make the 1985 team.

Tony told me, "If you give me half a chance, I'll pick you", but I wasn't able to give him that opportunity. He then asked me to help him out behind the scenes and I was only too pleased to do that.

I never felt like I was his vice-captain, I was more like his buggy driver. I helped him with the logistics of Ryder Cup week. I was never privy to what was going on in the team room; I kept out of the way of that.

Vice-captain is very much a modern term. Even when I asked Manuel Pinero to help me out for my first match in charge in 1991, we never referred to it as such. Manuel was like a bridge to the continental players for me, the likes of Seve, Olazabal and Costantino Rocca.

I enjoyed my time with Tony. I learned so much from him, the way he moulded the team and the way the players got behind him. There was never any dissent, anyone would play with anyone, there was a good balance and Tony was the inspiration.

We had a dominant team in 1985 and then again in 1987, but in 1989 we would have lost to the Americans were it not for the stunning two-iron at the last hole that helped Christy O'Connor Junior beat Fred Couples.

It was a tense; close match and you could sense the whole thing was going to be pretty close from then on. The United States are a tough nation, and they are never going to take too well to being beaten at anything over any length of time.

When I took over in 1991, there was a bit of a sea change going on. We were away from home, and it was always going to be difficult to succeed Tony at that point.

By 1993, for instance, Seve was not quite the player he once was and by 1995 he had lost his game and was more like an on-course captain in a way, an inspiration for the team.

I didn't have the best player in the world in my side anymore. Faldo was still there, though, and Langer too, but Lyle had also dropped off by then and Ronan Rafferty as well.

It was a big disappointment for me not to have Sandy or Ronan around for my first match as captain in 1991. They were great players and had helped to make exceptional teams under Tony.

Chapter 14
1991–2018 Review

1991 — KIAWAH ISLAND, SOUTH CAROLINA
USA: 14½, EUROPE: 13½

Bernard Gallacher took over as captain and asked me to assist him behind the scenes at Kiawah Island. I travelled to the Ocean Course in South Carolina in style — on one of the best-equipped private jets around.

I had been to Brunei a couple of times before to help the Sultan's nephew with his golf. A guy called Rafi Manoukian set up those trips and he and I flew out together to the 1991 Ryder Cup on his Gulfstream G5.

Everything on the plane was gold-plated and the seats were made of alligator skin. It was a luxurious way to travel, for sure.

I made a speech at the opening ceremony. I mentioned that it was time to hand the captaincy baton over to Bernard and I was out on the course for most of the time once the matches started.

There was no clubhouse at Kiawah then. Both sides used a prefabricated building to get ready and it proved very difficult to recreate the team-room atmosphere and unity we had enjoyed in the previous four matches.

The Gulf War had ended earlier that year and I didn't particularly like the way US captain Dave Stockton whipped it all up into such a frenzy that it was to become known as the 'War by the Shore'.

Some of the American players wore camouflage caps on the first day while Seve Ballesteros and Paul Azinger were involved in a confrontation similar to the one they were engaged in at The Belfry two years earlier.

Seve and Jose Maria Olazabal accused Azinger and Chip Beck of breaking the rules by changing their ball in the foursomes. The American pair shot back by complaining about Seve coughing in the middle of their swings.

It was all very unsavoury and got quite heated. After being told by the officials that no penalty would arise, Azinger muttered "Nice try" on the 10th tee as he walked past Seve's caddie Billy Foster.

Yorkshireman Foster passed on what the American had said and, well, that was like a red rag to a bull.

Billy said that Seve was absolutely raging, almost frothing at the mouth. He and Ollie were fully fired up by now and proceeded to win five out of the next eight holes to take the match 2 & 1.

I helped out Bernard whenever and wherever I could that week and it all came down to Bernhard Langer's six-foot putt on the last green of his singles match against Hale Irwin.

It was all on such a knife-edge, the tension was almost unbearable, and I remember Irwin saying later, "I couldn't breathe. I couldn't swallow."

Bernhard let out a cry of anguish when his effort slipped past the hole to give Irwin a half-point and the Americans a nail-biting victory. I felt badly for him and for captain Bernard, too.

Another player could have been destroyed by an incident like that. Not Bernhard. He showed what a great golfer he is and what a strong mentality he has by winning the German Masters the very next week.

1993 — THE BELFRY, SUTTON COLDFIELD
EUROPE: 13, USA: 15

Tom Watson was the US captain for the 1993 edition back at The Belfry and the spirit between the teams was far better this time, more akin to the way it should always be.

It looked good for Europe when we led by 7½ points to 4½, but Watson's men turned it around in the second day fourballs, winning the session 3-1 to leave things delicately poised ahead of the singles.

The Americans were on fire on the final day. Chip Beck rallied from three down to defeat Barry Lane, Ray Floyd produced another fighting display to beat Olazabal, while Azinger took a crucial half-point despite a hole-in-one from Nick Faldo.

I also recall Italian Costantino Rocca being particularly distraught after letting slip a one-up lead on the 17th tee to lose to Davis Love III.

1995 — OAK HILL COUNTRY CLUB, ROCHESTER, NEW YORK
USA: 13½, EUROPE: 14½

This was the only Ryder Cup I haven't attended in the past twenty-five years, and it was because I was involved in a busy schedule in my first season on the US Seniors Tour.

It went down to the wire again — just like the other two matches that Bernard presided over as Europe's captain. I was as pleased as punch that he got over the line this time.

This was Seve's last match as a Ryder Cup player and, although he lost his final-day singles 4 & 3 to Tom Lehman, the great Spanish matador gave another typical lion-hearted performance.

I've spoken to so many people who were at Oak Hill Country Club and it's amazing how they all refer to the way Seve could barely hit a fairway that day but, such was the awesome nature of his short-game skills, he was still able to give Lehman a run for his money.

1997 — VALDERRAMA, SOTOGRANDE, SPAIN
EUROPE: 14½, USA: 13½

Astrid and I stayed on the QE2, which was moored just off the coast of Sotogrande. It was yet another stirring tussle between two evenly matched teams and I was praying for Seve to win as captain on home soil.

By this stage, I was purely a spectator, but I spoke to some of the players, and they explained how much Seve was involved from the first shot to the last, even going as far as to tell his guys which clubs they should use at times.

That's how Seve was, though, always so excited and passionate about the Ryder Cup and burning with desire to defeat the Americans.

Rocca made amends for The Belfry four years earlier by pulling off a shock singles victory over the great Tiger Woods, who was making his debut in the event, and Colin Montgomerie topped it off by holing a long-range putt in the rain to halve his match with Scott Hoch and earn Europe a last-gasp win.

1999 — THE COUNTRY CLUB, BROOKLINE, MASSACHUSETTS
USA: 14½, EUROPE: 13½

It was crazy close yet again under Mark James's captaincy, but Brookline will always be remembered for the unfortunate incident involving Olazabal and Justin Leonard on the final day.

I was there watching it all unfold, and I know the American team were hammered for it, but I just think it was a simple case of over-exuberance from them.

In my opinion, no malice was intended when Leonard rolled in his 45-foot putt at the 17th and his teammates ran on to the green, stomping over the line of Olazabal's 25-footer. But it was an indication of how fragile the tightrope is between wanting to win and going over the top.

It also served as a reminder for future captains, if any was needed, about how animosity can so easily be stoked up between the teams.

If I had been in charge in those circumstances, I might have been tempted to concede Olazabal his putt, but it's not always easy to think as clearly as that on the spur of the moment.

Europe was 10–6 up going into the singles, looking dead certs for victory, but US captain Ben Crenshaw was made to look like a genius after his side staged a remarkable turnaround to win by 14½ points to 13½.

Crenshaw had given a spooky press conference the night before, wagging his finger at the journalists. He told them he was a big believer in fate and that he had a feeling that it wasn't over yet — what a premonition that turned out to be!

2002 — THE BELFRY, SUTTON COLDFIELD, EUROPE: 15½, USA: 12½

The Americans decided not to travel over for the 2001 matches because of the 9/11 terror attacks, so we had to wait another twelve months for the teams to return to The Belfry again.

There was a lot of ill-feeling after Brookline, but the additional year's gap gave everyone extra time to put things in perspective, while European captain Sam Torrance and US skipper Curtis Strange were both adamant in insisting that the matches would be played in the right spirit.

I was pulling for Sam, of course, and wanted very much for him to emerge a winner that week. He was always so passionate about the Ryder Cup and played under me in each of my four matches as captain.

He and his wife Suzanne had barely been married a year when the 1989 edition took place at The Belfry. It is almost the stuff of legend that I supposedly told Sam I would be getting him out on the course that week as much as possible in order to give him a rest!

I have to confess that I don't remember saying it, but, equally, Sam and I were always good pals and it's a cheeky line I can imagine I may have uttered.

Sam has always been an emotional sort. He wept after holing the winning putt for me in 1985, and when Paul McGinley did likewise for him on the very same 18th green at The Belfry seventeen years later, he was again unable to control the tears.

2004 — OAKLAND HILLS, BLOOMFIELD TOWNSHIP, MICHIGAN
USA: 9½, EUROPE: 18½

We all remember the matches at Oakland Hills for US captain Hal Sutton's gamble to play Tiger Woods and Phil Mickelson together on the opening day.

It's fair to say the guys ranked number one and number two in the world were not exactly bosom buddies. They've become much closer in recent times but back then it was a different story.

Sutton elected to combine two massive egos and it was bound to succeed or fail in spectacular fashion. They ended up losing to Colin Montgomerie and Padraig Harrington in the morning and to Darren Clarke and Lee Westwood in the afternoon.

There appeared to be precious little togetherness between Woods and Mickelson, Sutton's decision backfired, and it proved a massive boost for Bernhard Langer's European team.

I always found it peculiar the way the media hyped up Tiger's potential influence on the American team in those days. Don't get me wrong, he was a great player, but there is a limit to what he can do when it comes to the Ryder Cup.

Even if Tiger proves unbeatable on any given week, he can only contribute a maximum of five points to the overall effort, and the stats show that he has rarely punched his weight when it comes to Ryder Cup combat.

Again, there was no question about Europe's team unity that week and we prevailed away from home once more, Langer's men cruising to victory.

Sutton was pilloried for putting Tiger and Phil together. Hal and I have shared the stage for a couple of pre-Ryder Cup golf talks with some fans here in the States and he's always been pretty confrontational in those.

He believes the matches shouldn't be overly friendly; he stresses the fighting element and is quite aggressive with his opinions. But I'm not sure that kind of personality trait is conducive to good captaincy.

There was a big difference between Sutton's style and that of the under-stated but super-classy Langer. The German was very private about his strategy, and he bonded beautifully with his players.

I was chuffed for Bernhard that he managed to pull it off that week. He was always such a champion in all my matches in charge and I wanted nothing but the best for him.

2006 — K CLUB, STRAFFAN, COUNTY KILDARE, IRELAND
EUROPE: 18½, USA: 9½

Tragedy surrounded the 2006 matches at the K Club and I still find it hard to fathom quite how Darren Clarke was able to function as professionally as he did as a player, given the grief he must have been suffering following the death of his wife Heather just a few weeks earlier.

There was tremendous heartfelt support from the Irish fans towards him and the emotions of the week finally came out for Darren at the end when everyone started celebrating a runaway victory for Europe.

Golf is like a religion to those Irish crowds. They love their golf and the backing they gave Ian Woosnam's team that week was truly something to behold.

That was a unique Ryder Cup, and it was made that way by the galleries. I used to adore playing at the Irish Open in the Sixties and Seventies and I've always said those spectators are a special breed.

Woosie had a particularly strong side at his disposal at the K Club. It was as powerful a team as Europe have put together and I think it showed in the one-sided nature of the contest.

2008 — VALHALLA, LOUISVILLE, KENTUCKY
USA: 16½, EUROPE: 11½

Hal Sutton got it in the neck from the media four years earlier and this time it was Nick Faldo's turn.

I won't criticise Nick, he got enough stick from the journalists, but he had to play second fiddle at Valhalla to US skipper Paul Azinger who was lauded for his so-called 'Pod' system.

Azinger devised the plan to counteract the unity that was always evident among the opposition. He felt the Europeans were in natural pods because of the different nationalities in our teams so he tried to create similar close-knit groups within his side.

I recall Boo Weekley galloping down the fairway with his driver between his legs, the big-hitting JB Holmes thumping tee-bomb after tee-bomb and a vocal young Anthony Kim inspiring the American effort.

"I told you I was gonna whoop his ass," you could clearly see Kim telling his excited captain after crushing Sergio Garcia 5 & 4 in the pivotal first singles match on the final day.

Nick just happened to be on the receiving end of a damned fine collective show from the home team that week. I spoke for him when he was inducted into the Memorial Tournament's Hall of Fame at Jack Nicklaus's event in Ohio in 2015.

The cover of the programme is always dedicated to the honouree. It was a six or eight-page spread on Nick's glittering playing career and the headline at the top was 'Solitary Man'.

Nick was as single-minded as anyone has ever been in our game. That individualistic approach won him six Majors and it meant everything to him. He was as good as he always wanted to be — and who can argue with that?

He and I have always got on well; we are good friends to this day, and you'll never hear me say anything negative about Nick. The press loved knocking him throughout his career and it was hard to see him, and his players suffer at Valhalla.

On the positive side, we saw the emergence of Ian Poulter that week. He is like my 1985 Belfry hero Manuel Pinero, a great match-play performer rather than a great medal-player.

Ian has never won a Major; he has only three wins to his credit on the PGA Tour, but he's made his name on the back of the terrific performances he has produced in the Ryder Cup.

I'd go as far as to call him a match-play genius. He won four out of five points at Valhalla, and it paved the way for his staggering Miracle at Medinah exploits four years later.

2010 — CELTIC MANOR, CITY OF NEWPORT, WALES
EUROPE: 14½, USA: 13½

Rory McIlroy made his Ryder Cup debut at Celtic Manor in 2010 and a lot of flak came his way ahead of the matches after he described it as nothing more than "an exhibition event".

Once he stepped on to the first tee in Wales and heard the raucous cries from the galleries, he knew for sure that it was anything but an exhibition event, and fair play to Rory, he quickly admitted his mistake.

It also proved to be an error to stage the matches in the first week of October. The rain was incessant that week; the course became a quagmire; the fans were up to their knees in mud and the finish was delayed until Monday.

The Americans didn't have much experience of playing in those conditions. It favoured Colin Montgomerie's team, and they prevailed in another nerve-tingling encounter.

The course was purposely built to host the Ryder Cup, but the architects blundered because the final hole went straight into the setting sun at the end of the day and none of the players could see.

One of the cardinal rules of golf-course design is: Never build the first hole going east and never build the last hole into the setting sun. Whoever the designers were at Celtic Manor, they needed to go back to the drawing board.

Despite reeling off eight Order of Merit victories, Monty had never won any of the Big Four individual titles and he quite rightly described the Ryder Cup victory as captain as his "Major triumph".

It was also a memorable year for Graeme McDowell, who followed up his US Open victory at Pebble Beach by securing the winning point for Europe in his singles match against Hunter Mahan.

Thinking about the absurdity of the course set-up at Celtic Manor takes me back to an incident that occurred in the middle of my four Ryder Cup matches as captain.

I recall Turnberry putting in a bid to stage one edition and Lord Derby presiding over the outcome. Officials at the Scottish course produced a lovely red submission book presentation, but the British PGA chief looked at the cover and promptly threw it in the bin.

"It's all about the equinox, dear boy," he declared in that pompous manner of his, "we can't possibly go to Turnberry in September." He seemed to take great joy in making unilateral decisions like that and it was typically autocratic of him.

2012 — MEDINAH, ILLINOIS
USA: 13½, EUROPE: 14½

I was engaged in corporate hospitality for the 2012 event at Medinah, but I would happily have paid for the privilege of being there for that quite wondrous display by Olazabal's team.

The Europeans appeared to be heading for a battering at 10-4 down on Saturday afternoon, and it was at that point Poulter conjured five birdies in a row to set up the greatest escape of all great sporting escapes.

The Americans were still very much in control at 10-6 up going into the last day, but the leader board was a sea of blue for the singles, and it was bedlam when Germany's Martin Kaymer drilled in his seven-foot putt to ensure we retained the trophy.

Francesco Molinari's half-point in the final match against Tiger Woods meant Europe somehow contrived to scramble victory and Olazabal's reaction was unforgettable.

He looked up at the heavens, recalling his great friend and inspiration Seve — who had so sadly passed away a year earlier — and pulled his cap down over his face to hide the tears.

The team wore Seve's navy blue as a show of respect to the great man on the final day and also had his name emblazoned on their bags. Justin Rose pointed to the skies as if to say, 'This one's for him'.

Losing Seve was horrible but the memories of him in Ryder Cup combat would have been mentioned so often by Ollie and the players during that epic week.

If Steven Spielberg had scripted an ending like that, it would have been rejected for being too far-fetched for a movie, let alone real-life sporting drama.

It was an incredibly special occasion to witness. I remember walking a few holes with Astrid. The organisers said they limited the crowds to 20,000 per day, but there must have been 60,000 in attendance for the singles — the fans were pouring through the gates for hours.

2014 — GLENEAGLES, AUCHTERARDER, PERTH, SCOTLAND
EUROPE: 16½, USA: 11½

It was a telling year at Gleneagles. I thought the 2014 matches there perfectly summed up the difference between the two teams — the unity among the Europeans and the divisions among the Americans.

Phil Mickelson really did throw Tom Watson under the proverbial bus after the US captain had overseen a comprehensive defeat.

Mickelson has a reputation for saying it like it is and he referred to Watson's dictatorial approach. Perhaps the Americans erred by putting the eight-times Major champion in charge.

Tom was sixty-five then, at least one generation older than many of his players, two in some cases. It was like going back to the days of the old Great Britain team when we were captained by Bernard Hunt, John Jacobs and Dai Rees.

Tom had also been in charge at The Belfry in 1993. By 2014 he was less in touch with his players, and I don't think too many could argue that the age difference was a significant factor at Gleneagles.

Mickelson's post-match rant also typified how split the American camp can sometimes be. Tiger was absent in 2014 but his attitude to team events hasn't always been conducive to winning golf, and I think his ego played a big part in that.

He's a remarkable player, there's no dispute about that, but if his attitude is not what it should be, his individual abilities are no advantage to the team. The captain ends up carrying him to an extent and that's a definite negative.

Tiger has become much more team-oriented in the last few years, though. Look at the 2019 Presidents Cup outfit he captained — to my mind, that was the best an American side has ever gelled.

Paul McGinley was rightly lauded for his efforts as home skipper in 2014. He left nothing to chance in terms of preparation and even had symbolic European-blue goldfish in a tank in the team room.

It was gratifying, too, to hear Paul say after victory was clinched that he had used the Tony Jacklin captaincy template all week.

2016 — HAZELTINE NATIONAL, CHASKA, MINNESOTA
USA: 17, EUROPE: 11

Hazeltine National is a place close to my heart after the seven-stroke win I managed to achieve there in the 1970 US Open, and because I'm an honorary member of the club.

Davis Love III, who lost out to Olazabal at Medinah in 2012, was back for a second crack as US captain and he made sure he set up the course to favour the American players.

He cut the rough down to help his long hitters while the pins were stationed in the middle of the greens. Justin Rose was particularly critical of the less than demanding nature of the course after Darren Clarke's European team slipped to defeat.

I never went into the team-room that week, but I did play in a nine-hole Captains' Challenge ahead of the main event. Jack Nicklaus and I were the centrepiece of the opening ceremony, forty-seven years after the famous Concession at Royal Birkdale.

Darren's team lost at Hazeltine, but the fact of the matter is that if Europe wins every year, it becomes a no-contest. We got our butts kicked so often in the Sixties and Seventies that the matches almost died a death, so it's good that it goes back and forth from time to time.

Davis would have been a bit savvier after having wasted that huge lead at Medinah, while we had six rookies in our team, and I felt we made a mistake by not including the vastly experienced Paul Casey or the in-form Scot, Russell Knox.

The spirit of the matches was exemplified in the Rory McIlroy-Patrick Reed first singles match on the final day. That was a great Ryder Cup occasion, the two guys slugging it out like two boxers in a ring.

They played to the galleries too, which is the way it should be. Both men holed long putts on one green and walked off fist-pumping and laughing together. That's the sort of contest that draws the attention of millions of TV viewers around the world.

2018 — LE GOLF NATIONAL, PARIS
EUROPE: 17½, USA: 10½

Le Golf National outside Paris was as good a Ryder Cup venue as I've seen in all my years playing, captaining or watching.

I don't think you could find a better course; it was set up perfectly. The rough got progressively worse the more wayward the tee shot was, and that to me is one of the essences of golf.

I played alongside Paul McGinley in another nine-hole Captains' Challenge before the competition proper started and, despite being 74 years of age, I showed I can still do it now and again when I rolled in a nice 12-footer at the last to tie our match.

After Thomas Bjorn's Europeans had clinched victory, I remember a ridiculous Mickelson whinge. He said, "I can't play courses like that," but it was just the sort of layout you want for a Ryder Cup — one that rewards good shots and penalises the bad.

The players had to drive it straight, the pin placements were spot-on, and the huge grandstands were a welcome innovation. Thomas did a super job with his players and the team spirit among the Europeans was again first-class.

It was a memorable occasion for me because the general manager of Le Golf National is a guy called Paul Armitage — I used to sit next to his dad Geoff at school.

Geoff and his wife were there that week. He and I hadn't seen each other for years, so we had a lot of catching up to do, while his son Paul did a fine job with the facilities.

Thomas grabbed his opportunity to shine with both hands. He embraced the demands of captaincy ever so well and won his team over with his meticulous attention to detail.

The Ryder Cup is now in a wonderful place. I have to say that I'm pleased the matches were called off in 2020 because of the coronavirus pandemic because, without the fans, it would not have been the same.

I wouldn't want to see this much-loved sporting showpiece harmed for future generations by staging it behind closed doors. The noise and excitement among the galleries are an essential part of the whole experience — and long may that continue.

Chapter 15
Valderrama Ban

There was a period when Sam Torrance and I were both banned from playing golf at a now-famed Ryder Cup venue — a spell when my proud record as a player and captain seemed to count for nothing.

My late wife Viv and I were living in Jersey, but I'd already stopped playing professional golf and I was afraid of vegetating on the island — it's a dodgy place to get old with 70,000 alcoholics clinging to a rock — so we decided to move to southern Spain in the early Eighties.

I agreed a deal with a Filipino company that owned a golf complex in Sotogrande called Las Aves. We built a house by the 18th tee and the object of the overall exercise was to bring British and European companies over for golf weeks and golf days.

The course had been designed by the leading American architect Robert Trent Jones and I was playing on it all the time. I was also friends with the *Daily Express* owner, Lord Matthews, and I hosted the Daily Express Boys' Championship there — it was a perfect venue for the youngsters.

Everything was going well but it all suddenly changed when the facility was bought in 1984 by Jaime Patino, the president of a Bolivian tin-mining company.

The layout was redesigned and expanded by Trent Jones and became known as Valderrama. The new owner spoke of his ambitious plans and said it was his intention to turn it into the Augusta National of Europe.

But I quickly discovered how autocratic and unfriendly Senor Patino was and soon enough I received a year's notice that the course would no longer be available for me to play on.

While we were away on a short holiday, he built a road along the side of my house — a shortcut for his workmen to get to the maintenance area — which meant that at six o'clock every morning, we were woken up by the sounds of bikes and scooters instead of birdsong.

We owned two Dobermans and, one particular night, a gardener left one of the gates open and one of the dogs ran into the garden of a South American neighbour — a friend of Patino's.

I received a snotty letter telling me the dog had frightened their maid, but I was in no mood to take it lying down. I wrote back saying if their privacy was so important, they should erect a fence like most people on the complex.

Patino was informed and he instantly banned me and my son Warren from playing the course. Torrance, who was staying in Sotogrande at the time, was also banned after he was accused of filching from an orange tree in someone's garden.

In addition, Patino started to put up thirty-foot trees in front of some of the properties to make sure the owners couldn't see the course.

A few months later, I received a phone call from the European Tour to say that chief executive Ken Schofield and his number two, George O'Grady, would be coming down to Sotogrande with Mel Pyatt, a top official with Volvo.

They came round for dinner one night and told me they had some great news — that the Tour would be launching a lucrative end-of-season tournament at Valderrama called the Volvo Masters.

My instant response was to tell them that might prove difficult because I planned to write to every player and ask them to boycott the event due to the ban imposed on Sam and me.

"Oh, bloody hell!" was the reply. The three of them were in shock. They went back to their hotel and by mid-morning the following day I received a hand-delivered letter from Patino's secretary asking if I would meet him for tea at four o'clock.

I took the opportunity to write a two-page letter detailing all the grievances I had. I told him exactly what I thought of him, but if he still wanted to meet up for tea, he could get his secretary to call me.

It turned out that he still wanted the meeting to go ahead, so I went over. His secretary left us to it after pouring the tea, and Patino said, "Whatever happens within these four walls goes no further."

I reiterated what I told him in the letter, that he had made several accusations about my family and me that were untrue and that he had run roughshod over most of the people who owned homes on the complex.

He didn't really apologise, and I obviously didn't want to get in the way of the Tour, so he eventually decided to remove my ban. He listened to my criticisms and as I walked out of the door, he said, "You won't take advantage of this situation, will you?"

That was the last straw for me. I didn't like the man but had tried to come to a point where we could perhaps at least have a civilised relationship.

I replied, "You just can't help yourself, can you? Take it from me, I won't be stepping on your precious course ever again!"

A few years later, the Tour announced that the Ryder Cup would be staged at Valderrama in 1997 — the first time a home match would be held in Continental Europe.

I like to think I played a part in the decision. I told the Tour that we couldn't keep hosting it in the UK and that we had to pay due respect to Seve, Olazabal, Pinero, Canizares and Rivero — guys who had made such a great contribution to our recent successes — by taking the matches to Spain.

Seve, who of course went on to captain the team when Europe won in 1997, wanted the event to go to one of his local courses in the Cantabria region in the north of the country but Patino — who died in 2013 — made a financial guarantee to the Tour and Valderrama got the vote.

I actually played at Valderrama once or twice in the intervening years, but I never saw Patino again until we bumped into each other during the 1993 Ryder Cup at The Belfry.

I walked into the bar, where he was surrounded by a few of his cronies. He held his arms wide open and greeted me like a long-lost son.

We hadn't spoken for years but I shook his hand and said, "How are you, Jimmy?"

Referring to the Ryder Cup excitement going on around us, Patino joked, "Tony. Look at all of this — it's all your fault!"

Testimonial from Sam Torrance

Ryder Cup playing appearances: 1981, 1983, 1985, 1987, 1989, 1991, 1993, 1995

Ryder Cup captain: 2002

When Tony was made captain, he was revered by everyone on our tour. He had made a great impact as a player with his two Major victories — there weren't many players on our circuit who had that sort of CV in those days.

Then, as captain, he transformed the operation. When he got the job, he said he wanted to do it 'My Way', a la Frank Sinatra, and he brought in the leather golf bags, the cashmere sweaters, the Concorde travel, proper hotel rooms. It sounds like nothing, but those details suddenly made the players feel very special.

I learned so much from Tony as a captain. He was a great people-person; he was great with the whole team. He was always affable and for anyone who was struggling, he would almost mollycoddle them to sort them out.

One of the first things you experience as a player in Ryder Cup week is the motivational video. Three or four minutes of each player's best-ever moments are put together, and the whole camp sits there and watches.

It was superb for bonding, and I think Tony instigated that. It gives you great pride as an individual when great players like Seve, Faldo and Woosnam are sitting around watching you up on a screen — it certainly was something that gave me great pride.

The team room was an exalted place, it was always very special to be a part of, and that was something else Tony brought in. He would take questions and he would just sort the things out that needed sorting.

The main thing, though, was that he made every player feel so very special. His attention to detail was first-class. He made everyone feel good because he always took care of the little things, and all those little things add up to a big thing.

I remember Tony's assistant Bernard Gallacher delivering raw carrots to me out on the course at The Belfry once. Greg Norman at the time was saying that eating carrots was good for the nerves and I was munching them like Bugs Bunny.

That type of duty of care was typical of how we, as players, wanted for nothing under Tony's captaincy.

Chapter 16
Celebrity Friends

The Ryder Cup always attracted a host of big names to the matches, and I made so many celebrity friends as a result of those weeks.

Frank Sinatra, Princess Margaret, Burt Lancaster, Gerald Ford, Sean Connery, Andy Williams, Bob Hope, Bing Crosby, Jack Lemmon, George C Scott, Telly Savalas, Billy Eckstine, Peter Falk, James Garner, Glen Campbell, Perry Como, Buddy Greco, Howard Cosell, Arthur Askey and Frankie Vaughan were among those I shared some good times with.

Away from the Ryder Cup, I even experienced a game of golf alongside a US President when Gerald Ford and I teamed up for the old Four Stars European Tour event that was held on the outskirts of London at Moor Park.

That is something which has always struck me about the Americans — there's hardly been a president in office during my lifetime who hasn't been an avid golfer.

It's a great public relations boost when the most powerful man on the planet plays the game. We've not been as fortunate with prime ministerial golfers in Britain.

I remember Harold Wilson playing a bit in the Sixties and Seventies but most of our premiers have been cricket fanatics or lovers of other sports — and that doesn't help to keep golf up there in the spotlight.

It was a special moment when I met Sinatra for the first time. I've been lucky enough to have a bit of a singing voice myself and I made a couple of vinyl records back in the day.

I was playing at a tournament in Biarritz in the Seventies with my old Ryder Cup buddy, Peter Townsend. Sinatra was there and he and his entourage came out on to the course.

They stood behind Peter and me as we prepared to play our tee shots on one hole and it was an opportunity for me to go up and introduce myself to the great man, his wife and Jilly Rizzo, his famous minder.

I told them I knew Jim Mahoney well. Jim was Frank's press agent and he and I played together in the Bing Crosby pro-am event in California on several occasions.

We finished the introductions and, after the round had ended, Jilly came up to me at the hotel and explained that Frank had a DC9 parked up at the airport. He said they would all be leaving for White Plains in New York in the morning and Frank wanted to know if I wanted to join them on the flight.

I was also due in New York that week to play in the Westchester Classic PGA Tour event and of course, just like an idiot, I turned down their invitation.

I never met Frank again after that and it is a constant source of regret that I didn't take him up on the offer. I did have something of an excuse, I have to add.

In those days, if you didn't pitch up for the pre-event pro-am, you couldn't play in the tournament proper. I thanked Jilly very much for the offer but told him I had to leave that evening, rather than the following morning, to make sure I was there in time for the pro-am.

How I wish now that I had made an excuse to the Westchester organisers and taken up the once-in-a-lifetime chance of spending some precious time in the company of a man I admired so much.

I took my daughter Tina to a Sinatra concert once in the Eighties. Frank would have been in his late sixties or early seventies by then, but his voice was still as pure as the driven snow.

It was a great gig, and we thoroughly enjoyed the evening. I decided not to try and pester him backstage, or to remind him of our meeting in Biarritz but, boy, it was good to see him perform live.

As I said earlier, Jim Mahoney and I were good friends and I will never forget an incident that occurred back in 1974 when Jim got permission from Sinatra to come and watch me play in The Open at Royal Lytham, the venue of my breakthrough Major win of 1969.

Roone Arledge was the head of ABC Sports and a good friend to us all. His company were televising the tournament back in the States, Roone was in the ABC on-site trailer, and news came out that Sinatra had caused a storm in Australia after making some disparaging comments about the local women.

The Australians were refusing to refuel Sinatra's plane for his flight home, and he couldn't leave. He phoned up Lytham, asked where Mahoney was, and of course, Jim was with me.

Frank was angry that Jim was in Britain. "You should be here in Australia to help me out!" he fumed. He was famous for blow-ups like that, but he conveniently forgot that he had given Jim permission to be at Lytham that week.

Perry Como was another of the old crooners who was an avid golf fan. He lived in Jupiter, Florida and generally turned up for the Ryder Cup when it was played in the States.

I remember Tennessee Ernie Ford too. He was a well-known singer and television host back then. One of the highlights of his career came when he brought out the song 'Sixteen Tons'.

There were a couple of popular lines in that song like, 'You load sixteen tons and what do you get? Another day older and deeper in debt', and 'Saint Peter don't you call me 'cause I can't go — I owe my soul to the company store'.

We tried to get Tennessee up to do an impromptu number at one Ryder Cup, I recall, but he was a bit like Andy Williams because neither of them would do that sort of thing without perfect backup or accompaniment.

These guys — Tennessee, Andy, Perry — would rock up at the Ryder Cup for the whole week. They were all keen golfers, big fans of the sport. We gave them all the necessary credentials, and they were allowed inside the ropes for a close-up view of the action.

Rory Calhoun was a popular American film and television actor. He was known for his appearances in a lot of Westerns; he was another golf fan and used to follow me closely on the circuit.

Every year when I went to play in Los Angeles, I used to stay with Jim Mahoney who was always introducing me to stars like Rory. All these great entertainers were members of the exclusive Bel-Air Country Club and Jim had a spell as president of the resort.

Jim also came over for the BBC pro-celebrity golf series hosted by Peter Alliss at Gleneagles that featured Crosby and Connery as the team captains, with Johnny Miller and I as the professionals.

We used to play nine-hole matches in the morning and again in the afternoon. The big American stars used to come over, people like Burt Lancaster, Jack Lemmon, Robert Stack, Steve Forrest and Fred MacMurray — they all loved to play the game and pick the wits of the pros at the same time.

Burt was a great guy. I really enjoyed playing with him because he would have a mountain of anecdotes to tell. We would have dinner together in the evening too. For me, that was a real perk of the job.

He loved telling stories about Kirk Douglas, how the filmmakers of the day used to get his old pal to stand on a box to make him look taller, how he also put on high heels for certain scenes.

The British contingent was well represented, too: stars like Jimmy Tarbuck, Henry Cooper, Bruce Forsyth, Terry Wogan, Peter Cook, Tim Brooke-Taylor and my good mate Sean Connery.

Sean and I used to play together a lot when we were neighbours in Spain. He often tried to shock you out on the course, swearing in the middle of a situation when it was not justified.

He had his share of temper tantrums. He was a decent golfer; I think his best handicap was around seven, but he was the sort of guy you'd want to play with, not against.

The old adage says that golf shows up a man's character and Sean was a bit of a law unto himself. In the end, with him, I tried to stay out of it because I didn't really appreciate clubs helicoptering around.

But that takes nothing away from the great friendship we shared. He took care of everything when my wife Viv died out of the blue in 1988 — a real pillar of strength when I was at rock bottom and consumed by grief.

Sean was a mainstay of the BBC pro-celebrity series, which reminds me of an unforgettable incident at Gleneagles involving George C Scott when he drank a bottle and a half of vodka and cleared off the next day without playing.

He slept in a hospitality suite and the poor guy who was in charge of that area couldn't sleep because he was told that he had to babysit George throughout the night.

George slept on a couch, and when he eventually got up, the guy in charge tried to bring him around. When he was finally capable of stringing a couple of words together, he came out with the memorable quote, "There are only two things I want to do today: have a piss and get the hell out of here".

As he walked out of the door of the Gleneagles Hotel for the last time, the concierge shouted out to him, "What about your golf clubs, George?" He replied bluntly, "Burn 'em."

He then jumped in a taxi, and we never saw him again. All the newspaper men were around Gleneagles like flies but, of course, the rest of us had to keep mum. We weren't allowed to spill the beans.

It was like a long list of 'Who's Who?' in terms of the international stars that appeared in the BBC series.

It always used to surprise me when Crosby would walk into the dining room of the hotel without his toupee, and no one knew who he was. He was a stickler for never wearing his hat indoors.

I knew Bing well from all the appearances I made at his PGA Tour event in the States. The pro-am tournament used to be held at Pebble Beach, Cypress Point and Spyglass Hill — they were special venues, courses to die for.

Bing never sang on an impromptu basis, but I recall one night at Gleneagles when Connery stood up and belted out, 'Scotland My Hame'. The Scottish legend had some champagne in his hand, hurled the glass behind him and it smashed into small pieces.

The television companies don't do pro-celebrity series anymore because they simply can't pay these guys enough money to do them. The only comparable occasion is the new $10 million money-match between Tiger Woods and Phil Mickelson.

I also hosted a series just after the Loch Lomond Golf Club opened when I did my own interviews out on the course. My good pal Tom Weiskopf designed that spectacular layout; we picked nine holes for TV and the show went out on Channel Four.

Tom's fellow countryman Glen Campbell was the best celebrity golfer I ever played with. The singer was extremely good, a genuine two-handicapper.

Mind you, Bing was a skilful player, too, in his heyday. I always remember the opening nine holes we played at Gleneagles. He got on the first green; everyone was nervous, and we professionals had to calm down the amateurs as best we could.

We'd say, "Don't worry about the bad shots — if you hit any of those, we'll just edit them out."

Bing had the yips at the time, flicked at a six-inch putt and embarrassingly missed it.

It was a putt he had to make to win the hole and, unfortunately, we had no option but to tell him, "Sorry, that will have to stay in the edit." He understood the situation and was fine about it.

When Bing was at home in Pebble Beach, he drove around in a Rolls-Royce. He loved all things from the UK because he came from a time when Fred Astaire, Gene Kelly and the top American stars all revered the British way.

It was the Cary Grant film era they all adored. 'Ju-dy, Ju-dy, Ju-dy', they were drawn by that quaint accent, his way of speaking, and it was a fantastic time to be a popular Brit around those celebrities.

Phil Harris, who as a voice actor played Baloo in the 1967 animated film *The Jungle Book* and sang 'Bear Necessities', was married to actress Alice Faye.

He lived to the ripe old age of ninety-one. He and I used to get together every year, and the last time I saw him at Pebble Beach, Phil said: "If I had known I'd live to be 91, I'd have taken better care of myself."

The actors Jack Albertson and Peter Falk; the singer Billy Eckstine — he had a brilliant voice and sang 'Passing Strangers' — they all loved the game. Nowadays, unless you're a member of Bel-Air, you wouldn't know which celebrities play golf and which ones don't because most of them keep themselves to themselves.

James Garner was another who played a lot of golf. He starred in the motor racing film 'Grand Prix'. I sat next to him as we both watched it once, and he was giving me a heads-up all the way through as to what was about to happen in the movie.

You couldn't put a price on what it was worth to be around in those times and to be a part of the inner circle. One night, Mahoney, me and Howard Cosell, who commentated on all the Muhammad Ali films for ABC, went out to dinner with a guy who used to manage the Los Angeles Rams American football team — Don Klosterman.

Don had to walk around with the aid of a stick, but he was a tough guy. We drove past the home of the legendary jockey Willie Shoemaker on one occasion.

Cosell shouted, "Stop the car!"

We went up to the front of this huge house and into the intercom, Cosell roared, "Shoe, let us in!" The gates opened and as we strolled in, there was Tony Roma, founder of the restaurant chain.

We all sat down for a drink before Cosell bellowed, "Come on, Shoe, let's see all the silverware, then." We went into the trophy room and, strangely, there was a bed in there.

Willie, you see, was in the middle of a divorce and had clearly been kicked out of the main bedroom. He was a prolific rider of winners, and it was sad to see him end his days in a wheelchair after being involved in a car accident in 1991.

I played golf in Ireland with Robert Shaw — who played one of the lead roles in *Jaws* — at the Kerrygold Classic in Waterville in the Seventies. The two of us went out driving one night with his secretary, who he ended up marrying.

We stopped at a schoolhouse that featured in the Robert Mitchum film *Ryan's Daughter* before ending up in a pub. Robert refused to go in the posh area, so we ordered Guinnesses and sat down with a load of Irish guys wearing flat caps and with missing teeth.

I asked the locals, "Do you know who that is?" pointing at Robert. "Oh, yeah," came the reply. But they treated us just like one of their own gang and we had a great evening.

We stayed at the magnificent Waterville Lake Hotel. The owner, Jack Mulcahy, had tremendous clout and, all of a sudden one night, Bob Hope arrived with Bill Fugazy, president of the organisation that ran the Diners Club credit card company.

I knew Bill; we had met before at Bob's golf tournament in Palm Springs. I said, "Bob, I'll get up and sing for ten minutes if you get up and do a turn for ten minutes."

I sang the Johnny Cash number, '40 Shades of Green', and true to his word, Bob followed up by doing his stuff. That's the sort of thing that would be difficult to imagine nowadays.

We stayed in Palm Springs once for the Bob Hope Classic. The veteran comedian was asked about sex and violence, and he replied, "At my age, that's the same thing."

Richard Nixon went over one time and stayed near the Waterville Lake Hotel when he was US President — that gives you some idea how well-connected Jack was.

Jack introduced us to Frank Fitzsimmons, the American in charge of the Teamsters — the union that featured in *The Irishman* film starring Al Pacino and Robert De Niro.

Frank was among all these important top-brass guys sitting around a table at the Thunderbird Resort Club in Palm Springs — that was a picture I wish I'd taken, for sure.

Our British golfing celebrities were great fellows too. I'm thinking of Connery, Tarbuck, Forsyth, Wogan, Cooper and the likes. Henry was a really funny guy; he used to crease me up whenever we were together.

I remember telling Jimmy, Henry and Bruce a story about an eating contest in Toronto involving my golf mates Dave Thomas and Brian Barnes. In that strong cockney accent of his, Henry said: "I know a geezer who would eat you, you, you and you — his name is Nosher Powell."

Now, I knew the chap he was referring to because he hung around with Connery quite a bit. Nosher had an enlarged stomach and Henry said he never met anyone in his life who could compare as far as appetite is concerned.

I loved the way Henry used to tell his anecdotes. He was hilarious, even when he wasn't trying to be. "Yeah, yeah, yeah," he would say. Henry didn't laugh a great deal himself so that made him even funnier, I thought.

Tarbuck was another tremendous rib-tickler. We were all together once at a grand charity dinner during the Four Stars tournament he hosted with Forsyth, Wogan and Cooper.

We were at a table of ten that included Princess Margaret and Joan Collins, who was sitting next to her partner at the time, a guy affectionately known as 'Bungalow' Bill Wiggins.

Tarby was sitting next to Princess Margaret, who had no knowledge of Joan's latest flame.

"That gentleman sitting next to Ms Collins," she enquired, "who is he?"

"That's Bungalow Bill, Ma'am," replied Jimmy.

"And how did he acquire the name 'Bungalow'," asked the Queen's sister.

"Well, it comes from the fact he hasn't got a great deal upstairs, if you know what I mean, Ma'am," giggled Jimmy.

"And why is he sitting next to Ms Collins?" asked the Princess.

I shall never forget Tarby's reply.

"Well, Ma'am," he said with a completely deadpan face, "I think he is what is commonly known as giving her one."

To which Her Royal Highness replied, "Really, he must be very good at it."

Testimonial from Jay Monahan
(US PGA TOUR COMMISSIONER)

When I study the big picture of Tony Jacklin's life in golf, it is vibrant and rich in texture as he made history and enhanced the game as the most decorated British player of his generation.

And while Gary Player, Arnold Palmer, Jack Nicklaus and others are often credited as pioneers for competing around the world, Tony was certainly the most prominent European to do so, which included playing regularly in the United States, a rarity given all the challenges related to travel a half-century ago that we now take for granted.

His win at the 1970 US Open, the only victory by a European at that event between 1928 and 2009, is evidence of Tony's willingness to compete against the world's best.

But for many fans passionate about our game, it will be Tony's accomplishments and history with the Ryder Cup that will be best remembered. First as a player, and later as a four-time European captain, he led the charge in transforming a sleepy biennial team event that was being dominated by the United States into what we all now recognise as a global spectacle.

Without question, he paved the way for extended European success in the event from the likes of Ryder Cup giants Seve Ballesteros, Nick Faldo and Colin Montgomerie that continues today with Rory McIlroy, Sergio Garcia, Justin Rose, Jon Rahm, Ian Poulter and others.

Chapter 17
Royal Connections

I've been privileged to meet quite a few extraordinary people in my life and some of the best moments have arrived in the company of royals.

My first invitation to Buckingham Palace came in 1970 when I received an OBE from Her Majesty the Queen following my Open victory at Royal Lytham the previous year.

It was something of a double whammy that day because no sooner had the ceremony ended, and my late wife Viv and I were walking through the gates, that we were confronted by Eamonn Andrews holding his famous red book.

I was to be the subject of Eamonn's *This Is Your Life* TV show. Talk about a shock. After all, I was just twenty-five and so young—what sort of 'life' had I experienced by that age?

We were whisked off to the studio. Bill Shankland, the guy I worked under as a teenager at Potters Bar, was among the guests, some of my old schoolteachers, too. It was a surreal occasion and not something I had ever contemplated happening.

My mum and dad were there, Jimmy Tarbuck, and my great American golf friend, Bert Yancey. I was disappointed, though, by the absence of Fred and Maisie Baker, who put me up when I got the job at Potters Bar and were two people close to my heart. They took me in for a week, initially, in January 1962 and I felt so comfortable in their terraced house in Hertfordshire that I ended up staying for seven years.

Even after Viv and I got married in 1966, we always went back to Fred and Maisie's after returning from our golf travels. It was our base; there seemed little point travelling back to Lincolnshire and, if truth be told, I was barely on speaking terms with my mum. To get along with people, I have to like them. I don't share the belief that blood is thicker than water and my mum tried to run my life for too long.

Maisie was a great cook, she had a young son, we had a good social life in Potters Bar and her house was like a home from home for me, first, and then for Viv too.

The Bakers weren't invited on to *This is Your Life,* but it was a very special occasion for Miss Grass, my old schoolteacher. We took her to a London nightclub after the show and burned the midnight oil as a group.

I still have the red book containing my 'life' story that Eamonn handed me after the programme, and it serves as a poignant reminder of a magical day.

I went back to Buck House to receive a CBE in 1990. When The Queen presents you with a gong, she shakes your hand, talks for a while and then when she deems it time to move on to the next recipient of an award, she ever so gently nudges you to one side.

That was a formal occasion, but I also recall going to the palace for an informal lunch many years ago. Back then, The Queen used to host those types of functions around once a month, I was told, with six or seven different people from all walks of life invited.

I remember a publisher being there and a chairman of a big corporation. None of the guests knew one another but we were all being recognised for our respective achievements.

The Duke of Edinburgh and Princess Margaret were in attendance as well — my golfing accomplishments had clearly captured someone's imagination somewhere along the line.

I remember arriving at around 12.50 p.m. We had a drink and chatted for a while before going in for lunch. It was all over by 2.10 p.m., and I can still recall sitting in a daze in my taxi as I left the palace thinking, *"Did that all really happen to little old me, the humble son of a Scunthorpe steelworker?"*

I was always struck by the stunning opulence of the surroundings and by the way the uniformed guards stood in the corridors, none of them moving a muscle, with their glistening swords pointing to the heavens.

These are very rare occasions, something to soak up and treasure because they cannot be replicated. It's simply awesome to sample, albeit briefly.

I've been lucky to meet so many entertaining celebrities and sporting figures — people I hold in the highest regard — but no one comes close to The Queen. Her Majesty is, and always will be, my number one for the way she has conducted her duties and for the fact she has been a true inspiration to the ordinary working folk of Britain.

People often ask if I became nervous in The Queen's company. My answer is "No." I was simply really conscious of observing protocol in those circumstances, ensuring I did the right things and focusing hard on not making a bloody fool of myself.

After we retained the Ryder Cup at The Belfry in 1989, I went to a ceremony at the Ritz Hotel in London with my new wife Astrid to, ostensibly, pick up a prize from Princess Diana on behalf of the absent Nick Faldo, although I too received a surprise award for my captaincy achievements.

The princess and I were on stage when suddenly there was an electricity blackout. Diana didn't panic when the lights went out. She was as charming as always: she looked at me, I looked at her and it seemed as though we were both thinking, *"Now what?"*

Power was soon restored but Astrid told me that all she could hear from her table was Diana and I giggling together while the lights were out.

I mentioned the spectacular opulence of Buckingham Palace earlier and that was also a feature when Jack Nicklaus and I played golf in Morocco about twelve years ago with the son of the late King Hassan II, Prince Moulay Rachid.

We were both there on course-design business. The pair of us conducted a golf clinic and Jack did the talking while I hit the balls. Once it ended, a handsome-looking Mercedes arrived to whisk us away.

Jack asked, "Where are we going?"

I replied, "Don't ask me, I haven't got a clue."

Eventually, we arrived at a course in Bouznika that former US Ryder Cup star Billy Casper designed, and that the prince hadn't played on since his father died in 1999. Despite the fact that it hadn't been used for around a decade, the course was in pristine condition. The prince was hitting a few golf balls and he said to Jack and me, "Come on gentlemen, let's play."

The pair of us were without our golf shoes — in fact, any of our golf gear — but we went off in buggies and they started parading these breathtakingly attractive horses in front of us.

There were royal stables on the grounds and the grand nature of the facility was beyond words. The horses were housed in stunning stalls and the surfaces they walked on were like rugs. It could have been a scene from an epic movie production.

Jack was saying, "What should we do?"

I replied, "Let's just chill and go with the flow."

We played, we ate and then they brought out all the stallions so we could get a good, close-up view of these remarkable beasts.

The prince was charming and a perfect host. Our friendship remains to this day because every year I get a FedEx delivery from him. Inside a large envelope is always a much smaller envelope containing a signed letter wishing me continued happiness.

There are a couple of Tony Jacklin Golf Clubs in Morocco — in Marrakech and Casablanca — and I just have a wonderful relationship with the prince.

Ahead of the annual Hassan II Trophy European Tour event, a spectacular dinner for two thousand people is held in a huge marquee. The VIPs are presented to the prince before massive trays of food are served to row upon row of tables.

Astrid was with me the first time I attended, and we were both presented to the prince. My Norwegian wife was not introduced to him on the second occasion we were there and the pair of us became separated.

Neither of us knew what had happened but when we eventually met up again, we discovered that because Astrid had an American passport, royal protocol dictated that she could not meet the prince.

We got to our table, and I said, "Come on, let's go back to the room," and we walked out. But some officials scurried after us, urging us to change our minds. They were all extremely apologetic and we received a fantastic reception upon our return.

Astrid also played an important role when R&A secretary Michael Bonallack organised a trip to Buckingham Palace after my final match as Ryder Cup captain in 1989. We were invited to attend another special evening to commemorate retaining the trophy at The Belfry and Astrid introduced all the wives and partners of the players to Her Majesty.

It was another jaw-dropping function. These are the sort of moments that don't happen to normal people. We considered ourselves to be down to earth souls, even though we were all driven, single-minded golfers who had dedicated ourselves to our sport.

The Queen and the Duke of Edinburgh put everyone at ease. They must have known everyone was in awe and the two of them had a relaxed manner that helped make their guests feel as comfortable as possible.

Surprisingly, you never seem to get lost for words when engaging in chit-chat with the royals. It all seems to go smoothly, largely because of the easy-going atmosphere that's created.

In 1986, Viv and I were invited by Her Majesty to go to Windsor Castle for the official state visit of Spain's King Juan Carlos—that was another 'wow' moment among many 'wow' moments.

One-hundred-and-sixty-eight people sat at a gigantic banqueting table. The state visit was such a big deal back then that the BBC produced a one-off programme devoted to it.

It showed, among other things, how it had taken a week to set the table and how a butler sported two big dusters in order to clean the surfaces with his feet prior to the event, making sure everything was perfectly spotless.

Viv and I were part of the parade introduced to The King and we shook his hand before taking our seats for the banquet. We gazed up at the glittering chandeliers hanging from the ceiling and then down to a sea of Georgian wine glasses — each place setting had five of them!

It was comparable to dining at a seven-star hotel. I look back now and really have to pinch myself that I experienced an occasion like that first-hand.

There was such an absence of noise when the food was served that you could have heard a pin drop. It's tough to imagine but there was no clattering of dishes or cutlery — it all seemed to proceed like a military manoeuvre.

Margaret Thatcher and her husband Denis were present. The then prime minister was the daughter of a greengrocer and, like me, from a humble Lincolnshire background. Viv and I chatted with the two of them for a while before being seated and it was clearly evident how, in this exalted environment, Maggie and Denis were simple commoners, just like we were.

I hope this doesn't sound rude or demeaning but the prime minister did not appear quite so special in those surroundings, and it struck me pretty forcibly amid all that pomp and ceremony.

I mentioned the name of Rafi Manoukian earlier in this book. He was essentially what I would call a 'fixer' for the Sultan of Brunei.

I used to be quite a motoring aficionado in my younger days. On one occasion Rafi asked if I'd like to see their stock of cars and he took me to the Sultan's remarkable garage, which housed about two hundred luxury vehicles on two storeys.

There were Rolls-Royces, Bentleys and Ferraris all over the place. I remember Nicklaus visiting Brunei after me and the first thing he said about his trip was, "Did you see all the cars?"

I retired to my room one evening and Prince Hakeem said, "We'll call you when we want you." Rafi gave me a bunch of movies to watch before suddenly the phone rang at around ten-forty-five p.m.

"Let's play golf," was the instruction and out we went for eighteen holes on a floodlit course on the grounds, just the Prince and I. We finished at two a.m. and there was a feast of food and waiting staff ready to cater for our every whim; it didn't seem to matter that it was the middle of the night.

The Sultan had a whole host of English secret service guys. They clearly struggled to fill their days in a meaningful fashion and were all bored out of their minds. I talked to a couple of them, and they told me, "This is the last year we're doing this." But they were getting paid so much to do so little that they were empty threats.

There is a village-type facility on the island where the Royal Family host top people in sport. Prince Jefri, the Sultan's brother, was a good polo player and he used to entertain the best players from Argentina, for instance.

Prince Jefri also used to indulge himself by flying six-foot wide toy aeroplanes over the polo field. He was an Olympic-standard clay-pigeon shot as well and the two of us did that one day too, I recall.

Another time, the Brunei royals invited me to their English country estate, not a million miles from London. The house had some wonderful, curved windows that must have been worth a fortune. But the princes clearly thought nothing of it because they had a free-for-all paintball war game and started to shoot out the panes of glass.

When it was over, a huge box of McDonald's arrived — something like forty hamburgers — it was all so bizarre.

I did a few of these visits. I would be paid my fee at the end and, such was the generosity of the family, they would invariably throw in an expensive gift as well, maybe even a Rolex watch.

Ahead of the 1973 Italian Open in Rome, I was drawn to play with the exiled King Constantine of Greece in the pre-tournament pro-am. The two of us hit it off from the start, even though my long-time caddie, John 'Scotty' Gilmour, made an embarrassing faux pas on the very first green.

His Majesty was sizing up a putt when Scotty took hold of the pin and enquired, "In or out, King?" Luckily, he didn't hear the question, but I quickly went up to Scotty to admonish him.

I said, "Look, Scotty, you can't go referring to him as 'King'. It's got to be 'Your Majesty' or 'Your Highness'."

Scotty's reply was hilarious, and it had me in stitches. "Well, what do I know? I've never effing caddied for a King before!"

Anyhow, we all wound up having a really pleasant day and at the end of the round the King invited me to his residence in Rome later in the evening for dinner and asked me to bring five or six golf friends.

I recall asking Australian Jack Newton, among others, to join me there and one of my abiding memories was using a ladle to dish on to my plate some incredibly expensive Beluga caviar that, apparently, the Shah of Iran had supplied the King with.

There was so much caviar available from the buffet and I've never seen as much of it in one place at the same time before or since.

The King loved all the anecdotes and jokes that were being told and they got more risqué, and the night got longer. He said that he wished Prince Charles could have been there because he would have loved to share in the laughter.

A good time was certainly had by all that evening and an even better postscript was that I went on to win the tournament at the end of another joyous week on tour.

I've never met Prince Charles, but I did spend some time with his brother, the Duke of York, at an Open Championship held at the home of golf in St Andrews on one occasion.

In 2002, the most famous bunker in the game — the terrifying Road Hole sand trap on the seventeenth at the Old Course — was moved farther from the green and had two feet taken off its height.

The Japanese player, Tommy Nakajima, or Tommy Nakajimmy as he became affectionately known to the Scottish galleries, needed four strokes to get out of that bunker in 1978.

The Duke of York, who has always been an avid golfer, became captain of the R&A in 2004 and I remember walking him round St Andrews and getting to the seventeenth. I explained the changes that had been made to the greenside bunker, but he didn't seem terribly impressed with what I told him.

"I'm sure you are mistaken," he said. "It appears just the same as it used to be."

Never-to-be-forgotten days in the company of royals. Thinking back, it often feels like someone else's fairy tale.

Chapter 18
The Future

It saddens me to say so because I love the game passionately, but now golf has become boring for me, and I have little interest in watching it on television.

No doubt some will accuse me of sour grapes or of being a miserable old-timer who always thinks it was better in his day, but in my opinion and that of many of my contemporaries, the game's rule-makers need to bring back the distance the ball travels by at least thirty yards and also do something about the equipment being used.

Phil Mickelson stated not so long ago that the reason the modern players are belting the ball vast distances is that they are so much fitter than they used to be. I'm afraid that theory simply doesn't wash.

When I was in my pomp, I used to drive the ball around 260 yards, which was about average back then. I was physically strong; I wasn't a gymnast; I didn't put on any extra weight through my playing career, but nowadays, the players are hitting a five-iron that far!

You can't get away with saying it's down to the fact they all go to the gym because, in short, they don't. Twice Major winner John Daly never spent any time in the gym, and he propelled the ball a country mile.

You see guys now who are pencil slim, yet they smash their drives 350 yards. It's not about muscle, it's all about the ball and the equipment, and it's become insane.

The R&A and the USGA have dragged their feet for so long on these issues and it's time for them to act before it's too late. I have to confess, though, that I would be shocked if they did take a stance because there simply aren't enough people without bias in those organisations.

I don't think those two bodies have performed with much distinction in recent times.

It leaves me to wonder how much longer the US PGA Tour will allow the R&A and USGA amateurs to decide golf's rules. The PGA Tour is such a powerful entity, and it seems to me the time is right for them to take the bull by the horns.

You never see many organisational mistakes in regular PGA Tour events. Just look at this new rule about dropping the ball from knee height rather than shoulder height. What on earth brought that change on? What was wrong with the old rule?

And players can now wade into areas where a ball is lost or unplayable, and they can take practice swings, ground their clubs — anything goes. Players can also now putt with the flagstick in the hole. To me, they are messing with the game's history.

The distance the ball travels and the technology available to the players are the most pressing problems that need urgent solving, though.

I hope we get the right decisions made because it would then bring all those great courses back into the limelight that have been rendered irrelevant to the top professionals.

The pitch dimensions in all the other great sports like soccer, cricket and tennis are the same as they were a hundred years ago but, when it comes to golf, that's a different story because the courses are getting longer and longer to accommodate the increasing lengths the players are hitting the ball.

The likes of Jack Nicklaus, Gary Player and Greg Norman have been banging the same drum as me for decades and finally the R&A and USGA have woken up to the fact that we must curb the big hitters.

They announced the Distance Insights Project in 2019, saying they would examine distance through a multi-pronged approach that includes global stakeholder engagement, third-party data review and research.

But it's taken them so long to start addressing the issue; it could take them another decade to bring in solutions. By that time, the likes of Bryson DeChambeau, Rory McIlroy, Brooks Koepka and Dustin

Johnson will be in their forties and will have been overtaken by the next generation of elite performers.

I want sanity to prevail sooner rather than later and for something positive to be done to bring about the changes that will benefit the game in the long run because golf is simply not very interesting anymore; it's all about slamming the ball as far as you can, and about putting contests.

The players send it soaring into the distance, and it doesn't matter if they miss the fairway because even if they are in the rough and 100 or 150 yards short of the green, they just have a straightforward wedge in.

If they were hitting it fifty yards shorter and having to hit five-irons for the second shot, they wouldn't be getting the ball on the green from the rough.

The game is upside down with new technology. The modern players simply don't need it. It was brought in to help the amateurs, not the professionals, but I'm bound to think that the ball is the biggest culprit.

They're hitting nine-irons now where the top players were hitting five-irons fifty years ago. The courses are getting longer so it costs more to keep them maintained, and it means it takes so much more time to play.

I also don't consider that some of these elite guys are that talented and nobody looks like they're having a good time. They're all just going about their business. A thirty-foot putt goes in, but they don't smile; there's no fist pumping and it's all just very matter of fact.

The players have become too robotic. There's no emotion. Apart from the Ryder Cup, the guys these days don't interact with the galleries at all. It's the same people every week getting millions of dollars. Who cares anymore? It's all very predictable.

It's not like when Arnold Palmer or Seve Ballesteros were in their pomp. It used to be a real spectacle to see those charismatic players in action.

Tiger Woods, when he plays, still pulls the biggest crowds and he's got more oomph... but generally speaking, there's little emotion shown, and I don't think that's good.

Golf is at a crossroads, and I wonder how on earth it's going to move forward. The powers-that-be have lost the plot. The players shoot 61s and 62s as a matter of course every week, and it's making a mockery of the game.

They don't need fourteen clubs in the bag; they don't use half of them. It's crazy. And the greens are all perfect, they can tap spike marks down, unlike the old days.

If you had twenty-five putts a round in my time, it was a fantastic putting performance but they're regularly taking twenty-two and twenty-three these days.

There's no finesse to the game anymore. You don't see them fading or drawing the ball; it's all about gripping it and ripping it.

Tiger put it in a nutshell when he said the guys go for the driver every time. I always thought you had to hit the fairway to give yourself a chance with the second shot, but accuracy doesn't seem to matter now.

These guys are all swilling around in money; they take private planes everywhere but maybe that bubble will burst. I just don't think the people responsible for shepherding the game can see the consequences of their actions.

No one who truly loves golf could say this is a fantastic product that we have now. I don't blame the players for it. It all needs a big rethink from the top, but I don't think that'll happen.

There have been warning signs for years, alarm bells ringing. Palmer said the same for the last ten to fifteen years of his life, Nicklaus likewise, Norman, Player. But none of the advice has been heeded.

The R&A and USGA choose to go their own way and I don't think the game is better for it. All the wonderful golf courses that were 6,800 to 7,000 yards long, the Sunningdales, the Cypress Points, they would still be spectacular if they were played differently.

I played Cypress Point with double US Open champion Retief Goosen last year and he was driving the par-fours, at the age of fifty. You wouldn't dream of doing that before.

The way they've gone with the ball has made thousands of courses like that extinct worldwide. It's a smash-and-grab thing. A 7,500-yard course that used to be a renowned test is not a challenge to the modern guys because they're hitting wedges and nine-irons into the green more than fifty per cent of the time.

It's not a challenge nowadays; it's all very 'samey' to them. We used to read about Harry Vardon, Bobby Jones, Ben Hogan, the greats of yesteryear, but golf has gone so far away from what they all did, it's difficult to relate to the modern game.

Hogan's swing was a thing of beauty, and you watch guys today jumping off their feet. I'm fast losing interest in it. The game's not compelling to me any longer.

It is in a sorry state, and I'd like to see some of the old skills coming back; accuracy given more attention, more importance, rather than brute strength.

It's so predictable now. I can imagine some of these young guys thinking, 'Oh, he's just a moaning, whingeing old man'. But I just have the best interests of golf at heart because it's a game I've always loved.

Whether it's DeChambeau, Koepka or McIlroy, it's impossible to relate to how they are performing. I don't blame them one bit because, as a player, you take advantage wherever you can as you try to get in the winners' circle.

When The Open goes back to St Andrews in 2022, you are going to see 60 broken if the weather is fine. That surely can't be right.

Anchoring is another issue for me. It used to be a big deal to the rule-makers but suddenly it's not anymore. The players can do what they like. They are still anchoring, but it doesn't seem to matter now.

I'd like to see the ball go a maximum of 275 yards, but I think that's a pipe dream. There are so many decent players around these days. There never used to be when the equipment was difficult to use, we had persimmon heads, steel shafts and a ball that didn't travel as far.

You wouldn't get this mass of humanity being so good. It all needs rethinking, or someone needs to reinvent the game. We have to go back to the drawing board.

There is a yawning chasm between the game the amateurs play compared to the professionals. I'd allow the weekend hackers to use any new-fangled device they want if it makes the game easier for them, but for the pros, I'd rein back the ball to make sure golf was less predictable.

The game is so easy these days. The top players hit wedges and nine-irons into the green eight to eleven times a round.

Golf has become too one-dimensional but if the professionals, i.e., the PGA Tour, started making the rules, it would be a different game, I'm sure.

Glenmorangie
The book sponsors

I've always been a great believer in timing, and, as far as my lengthy association with Glenmorangie is concerned, the timing has always been perfect.

Back in 2011, I heard that Glenmorangie was going to be associated with The Open Championship — a golf tournament that is very dear to my heart.

I've been a devotee of the fine single malt Scotch whisky — I have a particular penchant for the original brand — the company produces for a long time, and, as a former Open champion too, the link with the championship seemed an opportunity to arrange a marriage made in heaven.

I decided to send my then-representative to Glenmorangie's headquarters in Edinburgh straight away for a meeting to find out if there was a way that we might be able to agree some form of alliance.

At the same time that meeting was taking place in Scotland, I played in a pro-am golf event close to my home in Bradenton.

When I arrived at the pro-am, the organisers said they would be pairing me up with a VIP — and by a strange quirk of fate, that VIP was Jim Clerkin.

As I was soon to discover, Jim just happened to be the president of Moët Hennessy, USA, owners of the Glenmorangie brand.

Jim and I hit it off and, in the unforgettable words of Humphrey Bogart in that classic black and white 1930s movie *Casablanca*, it was 'the start of a beautiful friendship'.

The two of us struck a deal on a partnership and I was soon to become Glenmorangie's Global Ambassador.

We've shared some memorable times together over the decade. I've met some fabulous people who work for, and are associated with, the company.

Glenmorangie is a great company, and I am proud that they have decided to reinforce our partnership by agreeing to sponsor this book, *Tony Jacklin: My Ryder Cup Journey*.